HOW TO DRAW
DIGITAL CARTOONS

A STEP-BY-STEP GUIDE WITH 200 ILLUSTRATIONS

FROM GETTING STARTED TO ADVANCED TECHNIQUES, WITH 70 PRACTICAL EXERCISES AND PROJECTS

IVAN HISSEY AND CURTIS TAPPENDEN

WITHDRAWN
southwater

This edition is published by Southwater, an imprint of Anness Publishing Ltd,
Blaby Road, Wigston, Leicestershire LE18 4SE

Email: info@anness.com

Web: www.southwaterbooks.com; www.annesspublishing.com

If you like the images in this book and would like to investigate using them for publishing, promotions or
advertising, please visit our website www.practicalpictures.com for more information.

Publisher: Joanna Lorenz
Editorial Director: Helen Sudell
Editor: Elizabeth Young
Cover Design: Oil Often
Production Controller: Bessie Bai

Designed and produced for Anness Publishing by
The Bridgewater Book Company Limited
Project Editor: Polita Caaveiro
Designers: Jan Lanaway, Kevin Knight, Steve Knowlden
Art Director: Lisa McCormick

Ethical Trading Policy
At Anness Publishing we believe that business should be conducted in an ethical and ecologically
sustainable way, with respect for the environment and a proper regard to the replacement of the
natural resources we employ.

As a publisher, we use a lot of wood pulp in high-quality paper for printing, and that wood commonly comes
from spruce trees. We are therefore currently growing more than 750,000 trees in three Scottish forest
plantations: Berrymoss (130 hectares/320 acres), West Touxhill (125 hectares/305 acres) and Deveron Forest
(75 hectares/185 acres). The forests we manage contain more than 3.5 times the number of trees employed
each year in making paper for the books we manufacture.

Because of this ongoing ecological investment programme, you, as our customer, can have the pleasure and
reassurance of knowing that a tree is being cultivated on your behalf to naturally replace the materials used to
make the book you are holding.

Our forestry programme is run in accordance with the UK Woodland Assurance Scheme (UKWAS) and will be
certified by the internationally recognized Forest Stewardship Council (FSC). The FSC is a non-government
organization dedicated to promoting responsible management of the world's forests. Certification ensures forests
are managed in an environmentally sustainable and socially responsible way. For further information about this
scheme, go to www.annesspublishing.com/trees

Previously published as part of a larger volume, *The Practical Encyclopedia of Cartooning*

Acknowledgements
The publisher would like to thank the following for kindly supplying photos for this book: Dell Inc. 7tl;
Canon UK Ltd 7tr; Epson (UK) Ltd 7tm and ml; Wacom Europe GmbH 7mr.

All other artworks by Ivan Hissey

A big thank you to Jane for her enthusiasm and support, and to Curtis for his stamina and constant cheerfulness.
Ivan Hissey

Thanks to all who encouraged and supported the making of this book. Firstly to Ivan Hissey who provided
outstandingly versatile artwork with true professionalism, making my challenge as author so much easier and very
enjoyable. Thanks to Susanne, my wife and manager, for encouraging me throughout and keeping it all on track.
To my children, Tilly and Noah, for their enthusiasm and wonderment as the project unfolded – with special
thanks to Noah for trying out many of the cartoon exercises! *Curtis Tappenden*

CONTENTS

Digital techniques

Cartoons like all other artistic expressions have embraced the digital world. Far from making drawing skills redundant, they have blended them with diverse imagery programs to increase visual possibilities. This section explains the development of software, and how to use it appropriately and successfully.

The digital environment

Digital media has revolutionized the world of art and design. Before the advent of computing, processes such as changing colours, making adjustments and alterations, duplicating and archiving artwork required much extra effort. In addition, effects such as seamlessly smooth colour gradations were time consuming and demanded the skilful use of a very fine brush or airbrush. Now these things and more are easily and quickly achieved using single keystrokes and mouse skills.

Digitally created imagery is constructed from pixels – tiny, flat squares of colour, which are neatly duplicated in rows of thousands or millions to give an accurate, crisp appearance.

It is the perfect medium for creating flat, polished graphic art, and can be easily combined with traditional methods where a more textured or fluid style is wanted.

The advantages of using the computer are the ease with which minor changes can be made to pictures and the extraordinary provision of having artwork ready for publication as digital files, be they comics, books or websites.

While digital software packages greatly assist basic drawing and painting skills they can never replace them, and all artists who produce computer-generated artwork are invariably grounded in these traditional skills.

Vector and bitmap

There are two principal types of digital imaging programs. Vector programs use mathematical algorithms (a language known as Postscript) to describe colours, lines and curves. A Pen tool existing in an on-screen 'toolbox' plots a series of lines and curves with points connecting each

section of the line or curve. The areas can be filled with colour and 'stroked' by altering the line thickness or its colour. Vector programs, such as Adobe Illustrator and Freehand, allow the user to create complex drawings. With 'Bitmap' or paint programs, such as Adobe Photoshop,

users draw freely on screen using a mouse, stylus pen or drawing tablet. The smallest unit of computer storage – a 'bit' – is mapped on to a grid. An image that is created or scanned-in is displayed on-screen as an arrangement of bits. Such files can take up a lot of memory.

Bitmap digital photograph ▼
This digital photograph of a guitarist is a bitmap image of 300dpi (dots per inch is a term denoting screen and print resolutions). It is imported into the vector program Adobe Illustrator, where it acts as a base template.

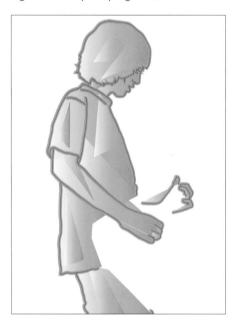

Vector digital drawing ▲
The Pen tool is selected from the toolbox palette in Adobe Illustrator and used to draw the outline around the guitarist. Vector and bitmap programs use 'layers', which are the digital equivalent of transparent overlays. Each layer can be allotted to a different portion of the illustration, such as outlining, colouring and textures. Here, the outline has been copied to a new layer and the gradient added in order to blend the red into the yellow.

Bitmap digital painting ▲
The vector digital drawing is 'cut, copied and pasted' into Adobe Photoshop, the bitmap program that manipulates images. The layered Illustrator drawing is partially removed around the guitar section of the image beneath using a selection of toolbox brushes. The Photoshop file of the guitar will appear as another layer – as parts of the top layer are removed or altered, the image on the layer below appears, as though someone has physically cut through a mask or tracing paper. The background is painted blue and a halftone filter is applied, then partially erased from around the figure.

Digital equipment

Digital artworking requires high-specification equipment. You will need a powerful Apple Macintosh computer or Microsoft Windows compatible PC, plus a high-definition monitor with a screen at least 15 inches wide. As well as a mouse, pen or graphics tablet and software, a desktop scanner capable of scanning line and halftone images and a colour inkjet or laser printer are essential. A back-up device or external hard drive is also very useful for storage.

Digital camera ▼
It looks like a conventional SLR or instant camera, but instead of capturing the image on light-sensitive film to be developed, it converts its picture into a form that can be downloaded and stored on your computer.

Computer and monitor ◀
Most computers now house dual processor chips of at least 500MHz, which is powerful enough to deliver 7 billion calculations per second. Most monitors are LCD flat display panels with 1600 x 1024 resolution.

Digitizing tablet ▼
They are useful, some say essential, for making digital pictures. With a cordless pen-like stylus, the artist presses on to a flat, plastic tablet and the 'drawn' movements correspond with that of the cursor on screen, graphically displaying the result.

Printer ▶
Laser printers, such as Epson's EPL 6200, use reflected light and static electricity to deposit toner on to the paper, while inkjet printers spray microscopic jets of electrically charged droplets of ink deflected by electromagnets on to moving paper.

Scanner ▲
Desktop scanners, such as Epson's Perfection 3590, allow artists to input images already created into a computer format – the bitmap – for further manipulation or reference purposes. The most common scanners are flatbed of A4 size, allowing an image of that size to be laid and copied.

Conventional versus digital imagery

The question of whether traditional or digital methods of image-making are better will always be governed by the results you are looking for. So long as the final image is well executed and fits the brief you have set, it really does not matter how you go about creating it. However, certain styles or effects are better achieved by one or the other medium. A cartoon consisting of flat colour or soft blends is less painstaking to create on the computer than by hand, whereas a rough textured look or mixed-media collage work to best effect using traditional methods.

Traditional drawing ▲
The leopard is drawn by hand using a dip pen and black Indian ink. The very lively line is due to the changing delivery of the ink flow controlled by the nib.

Vector-based drawing ▲
This drawing was made with the Pen tool in Adobe Illustrator. The line quality is slightly lighter although extra points were added to give the effect of pressure.

Vector-based colouring ▲
Still in Adobe Illustrator, the Brush tool was set at various sizes to add colour on another layer. A gradient was applied to form the smooth brown to yellow blend.

Essential software

Your computer hardware needs the right design software to activate it and enable you to get creative. Before purchasing software, check that it is compatible with your computer's operating system. This is Microsoft (Windows) on a PC and Apple (OS) on a Mac and they are totally different. Most application software is available in CD-Rom format or can be downloaded from the Internet. All versions are named or coded to differentiate the new from the old. Sometimes Internet 'updates' are available supplied free from the manufacturer, not requiring you to buy the latest versions. However, newly developed packages are often much improved and it may be better to purchase these instead. If you are planning to submit your cartoons for publication, it is essential to be aware of the version you are operating to ensure compatibility with a client or recipient of your work.

The cartoons in this book are created using the drawing and painting programs Adobe Illustrator, Adobe Photoshop, Corel Painter and the animation programs Flash and ImageReady.

Drawing and painting programs

Adobe Illustrator and Macromedia Free-hand create vector images and are known as 'draw' programs. These programs are mathematically devised through the accurate plotting of points. Joined points form a line and joined lines form a shape to which flat colour can be applied. The format of this program results in images which look crisp, slick and clean. Adobe Photoshop and Corel Painter are 'paint' programs and, as this suggests, employ a more freehand style of picture creation. They construct pictures using individual 'bits' which replicate textures familiar to the traditional artist.

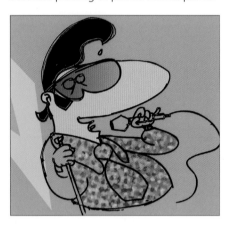

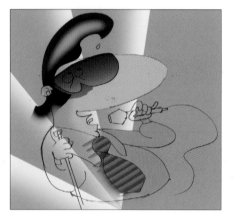

Adobe Illustrator image ▲
Like all 'draw' programs, Adobe Illustrator has close links to page-layout applications. The Illustrator tool kit allows boxes, ellipses and curves to be drawn. Pictures are created using an on-screen Pen tool by connecting points along so-called Bezier curves. When two points connect, a line is formed with new 'handle' points that can be pulled out to curve or change the direction of the line.

In addition, scanned images can be imported and 'traced over' and Illustrator is excellent for manipulating type. The layering feature enables image sections to be edited separately, and stretching, skewing and rotating are all possible. Although the skill of dragging handles out from points takes practice, the advantage of this program is that it creates complex images with very low file sizes which hold their sharpness even when enlarged.

Adobe Photoshop image ▲
This 'bitmap' program was first developed as a photographic retouching tool, which rendered the manual airbrush obsolete. A user-friendly application, its vast scope and flexibility mean that it is recognized worldwide as the industry standard for retouching and art creation. Pictures are made by physically moving a mouse or stylus pen and the program gives the user access to a huge range of tools, techniques and effects. As with Illustrator, the system of working in layers gives the freedom to experiment and rework.

A major asset of Photoshop is its ability to manipulate, retouch or recolour digital pictures, whether uploaded from a camera, downloaded from the Internet, scanned or 'grabbed' as a screenshot from a DVD. In addition, final images can be converted into a range of file formats that are compatible for use in other applications or systems.

Corel Painter ▲
This program emulates traditional paint effects, such as watercolour, pastel, oils and acrylic. The program's extensive range of brush palettes are specifically geared to the sensitivities of the traditional artist: they range from soft round or flat watercolour brushes to firm bristle varieties for dabbing and stroking on acrylic and oil paint. The ability of the pressure-sensitive stylus pen to create corresponding marks on-screen is another feature which makes it attractive to the traditionalist. The system of layers enables changes to be made quickly and easily.

Although bitmap programs are easier to use than vector-based applications, image file sizes are usually large. However, all digital files can be saved in other formats for sharing and a full-colour A4 image of about 34MB can be compressed without too much distortion.

Making an image using more than one program

Each program has cornered its own niche, whether infinitely scaleable illustration, digital image manipulation or the reproduction of natural media. While you can approximate many specialized features with just one program – such as painting digitally with Photoshop – combining different approaches can lead to startling and original fusions of artwork. Creating such composite images couldn't be easier, as today's programs are designed with mutual compatibility in mind. You can import a vector-created design into a bitmap program, such as Photoshop, by dragging the vector image into a new document window or opening it with the application. Either way, it will appear as a new layer in the layers box. From this point on, further work on the vector image can only be applied using Photoshop. The advantage of the layered system of working is that it allows you to adjust individual sections of your illustration and move them between applications, playing to the strengths and different styles of each program.

Illustrator ▲
The flat artwork for the hands and trousers is created in Illustrator, but the shoes, bottle, drinks carton, shirt front and tie are sourced from magazines and scanned.

Photoshop ▲
The various textures and patterns of the shirt and tie are created using Photoshop's style palettes. They are selected and built in layers.

Painter ▲
The strong tonal image of the head is created in Painter using an acrylic paints palette and Brush tools. The smooth almost buttery texture is worked using the Blender tools.

Scanned image ▲
The cake is a scanned photo imported into Photoshop with an airbrushed-effect drop shadow. The flat table artwork is an Illustrator creation.

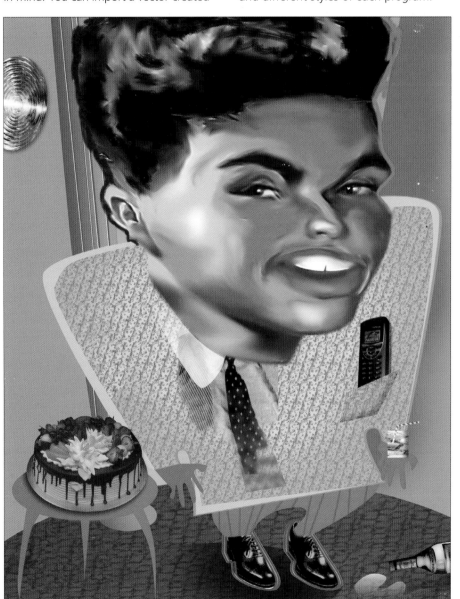

Painter, Photoshop and Illustrator ▲
This caricature is created using Painter, Photoshop and Illustrator applications. The composite image was made in the two vector programs and finalized in Photoshop. Its composition reveals the level of compatability between the three programs and is proof of the pixel's ability to unite different styles and techniques, textures and colours.

Scanning an image

You can input 'real' pictures, such as magazine cut-outs, and convert them to digital images via a desktop scanner, all of which come with their own scanning software. This connects to the computer via a USB port or via a faster, high-speed interface known as Firewire. Although more expensive than A4 size, most artists prefer the flexibility of an A3 size scanner. There is no limit to the types of images that can be scanned and photos, transparencies, halftone illustrations or line drawings will all maintain their original quality. As a general rule, images are scanned at a resolution which is double the size of intended use. So an image scanned at 300dpi (dots per inch) will reproduce a sharp on-screen or printed image which is 150 lines deep. In general, the greater the number of dots, the greater the intake of information and the better the quality of an image.

Scanning a line image

The method for inputting an image is similar with most software packages. There is the opportunity to select a 'cropping' area and to pre-scan and preview your work before finally copying it on to your computer. You will also have the chance at any time of recropping in the program you have chosen.

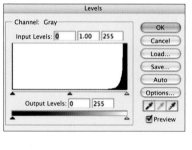

Scanned levels

On screen ▼
Once scanned, the image should be opened in Photoshop or equivalent bitmap program for further tidying. Adjusting the Levels settings (Image > Adjustments > Levels), and sliding the histogram sliders to the left, brightens the scan and removes unwanted dirt or pencil graphite. The sliders in the Levels box are known as 'end dots' of a print screen and are the very darkest and lightest tones visible. Moving the right-hand slider too far to the left, deletes the lighter dot.

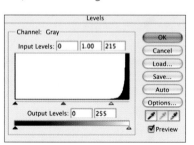

Pre-scan and scan ▲
Once the image is pre-scanned, there is the opportunity to adjust the settings before scanning for real. For example a blacker line could be achieved by setting Auto Exposure Type to 'Line'. The maximum resolution size is set at 600dpi because it can be reduced later on.

Tip: It doesn't take a lot of technical know-how to adjust scans. Try out test pieces and play with the histogram sliders on the Input and Output levels and see what happens to your image. Only hit the OK button when you are satisfied with the result.

Adjusted levels

Tidying a scanned image

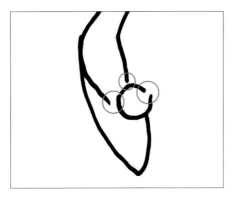

Repairs ▲

If your grayscale scan has 'broken' – a piece of line isn't strong enough to hold colour or has become thin and 'brittle' in the scanning process – you can use the Pen tool to strengthen the line or strengthen the offending segment by multiplying it. Select the area using the Lasso or Marquee tools in Photoshop, then copy and paste the line over the broken area on a new layer and set to 'Multiply'. When you're content with your fix, flatten the image (Layer menu > Flatten image) to reduce it back to a single line drawing.

Hue and saturation ▼

It is possible to change any part of any line by first selecting it with the Marquee or Lasso tools and then adjusting the colour or density values using the Hue/Saturation sliders (Image menu > Adjustments > Hue/Saturation). Experiment on a tester before making the final changes to your artwork, as this will assist your thinking processes and save you time in the long run.

Refining ▲

Use the Zoom tool to check for areas from the original drawing that need refining. Use a 3-pixel brush (solid, not feathered) to retouch the area. Keep in mind, you have multiple levels of undo.

Image inversion ▶

To check how clean a scanned image is convert it into negative (Image menu > Adjustments > Invert). It should have a solid white line and no speckling.

Image proportions ▼

Any image or part of an image can be reduced or enlarged using Transform (Edit menu > Transform). If you want proportionate scaling, remember to hold down the shift key while resizing it or it will distort as can be seen in the middle figure below.

Colouring a scanned image

The beauty of adding colour to an image in Photoshop is that you can make as many changes as you like on numerous layers without affecting the original. Any colour or painting technique that you no longer wish to display is simply deleted.

The range of colouring effects and application methods of this program can be overwhelming for the beginner. The best way to learn is by experimenting, safe in the knowledge that provided you work in separate layers, nothing will be lost. This learning process is common to all artists: it helps them to pin down working methods and define drawing styles.

This practice exercise shows you how to set varying levels of colour tones to suggest highlights and shadows, and even add some textures into the mix, which are essential if an image is to have good overall balance.

Practice exercise: Adding colour, tone and texture

Transforming a flat single-line drawing into full-colour 3-D artwork is a simple process that gives a stunning result. The 'hands-on' experience of working in multiple layers allows you to take a logical step-by-step approach. Expect slow progress while you are learning to use and control the various tools, safe in the knowledge that your speed will pick up as you grasp the technical know-how. It is always better not to rush through, but gain understanding carefully, even if this means taking extra time.

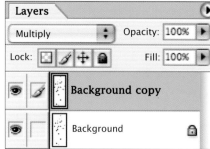

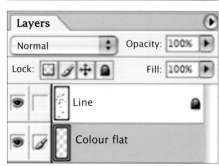

Tip: The layers panel has a lock, eye and brush icon. 'Locked' images cannot be worked on – scanned images are locked automatically as layers until you add another layer. To separate out your line work and begin colouring, copy your locked image with the 'Duplicate Layer' command. Use the Magic Wand tool, with 'Contiguous' unchecked, to select all areas of white on your image and delete them. Meanwhile, delete the original background layer, which will become unlocked – use this to add your colour, working *behind* your untouched black lines. Clicking the eye icon makes a layer visible or invisible – useful for checking your compositions, isolating layers or testing out filters. The brush icon shows which layer you are currently working on.

1 The line drawing is scanned as a bitmap 600dpi 'Grayscale' image (Image > Adjustments > Grayscale). To add colour it will need to be converted to a colour image (Image > Mode > RGB Color) and then significantly reduced in size. Go to Image > Image Size > Resolution and adjust Pixels/Inch in dialogue box to 300dpi. You are now ready to start colouring.

2 Duplicate the line image as a new layer with the 'Duplicate Layer' command or copy and paste the entire image. It will automatically appear in the layers palette. Change 'Normal' to 'Multiply' by scrolling down. Now click on the original background layer and delete it so that the new layer is now the colour layer. Label the specific layers to avoid any chance of confusion.

3 Apply flat colour with a 'flat' 100–200 pixel brush. You can access Colours either by clicking on a square in the toolbox that offers a colour palette or from the colour palette or colour slider bar on the desktop. If your colouring goes over the lines, simply clean around the line on the Colour flat layer with the Eraser tool (toolbox palette). The outline has its own layer and rests intact.

4 Create a new layer, position it above the Flat colour layer and label it 'Shading', as the screengrab shows. Select the areas to shade with the Magic Wand tool (toolbox palette). Select the shading layer and add 15% black to your original colour. Apply this shade colour using a soft brush.

5 Create a fourth layer and label it 'Highlighting'. To make new colours in the same hue range, simply reduce its strength by 20% and it is significantly lightened. Lock the other layers and select a soft brush to add the highlights. Experiment to see what effect you get by altering the colour Opacity, for example.

6 Create a 'Texture' layer and lock the other layers. Select within the outlines of the bag and strap and add the texture from the Filter menu (Filter > Texture > Craquelure). Select a different texture for the dress. Once areas are selected and made as new layers, you can experiment with textures and patterns.

Making colour changes

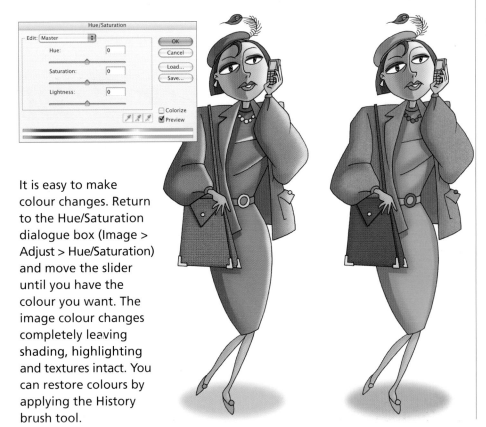

It is easy to make colour changes. Return to the Hue/Saturation dialogue box (Image > Adjust > Hue/Saturation) and move the slider until you have the colour you want. The image colour changes completely leaving shading, highlighting and textures intact. You can restore colours by applying the History brush tool.

Colouring comic artwork

A common process for digitally colouring comic book cartoons is to build layers of flat colour beneath the original 'line' layer of a scanned-in ink drawing. The highlights and shadows are applied using the methods shown on these pages, and the areas around the lines neatened with the Eraser tool.

The vector drawing program

The benefits of a vector drawing program, such as Adobe Illustrator, are most clearly seen when it is the sole program used to develop a sketch from draft to final colour artwork. It produces digital images in a distinctly slick style that combines crisp, clean lines with smooth flat colour. It by no means produces quicker results than other programs – in fact, creating shapes with the level of accuracy offered by a vector program can take time as you meticulously plot points, but as with all skills you will get quicker with practice. Another key advantage to using a vector program is that it uses far less memory than a bitmap program, so there are fewer problems with opening or storing images. This gives you the freedom to work on large-scale illustrations or on sequences, such as comic strips or cartoon narratives.

Practice exercise: Creating a vector cartoon

Computers cannot replace artistic skill when it comes to creating images. They are an excellent tool but their only role is to respond to logical commands. Traditionally, an artist will 'think' and redraft a composition many times on paper and thinking remains a vital part of the process of refinement for a successful outcome. Using a computer program instead of paper changes nothing except that it is generally a speedier process. Create a file for the storage of sketches so that you can access them with ease and efficiency at any time.

> **Tip:** Name each layer you create for ease of use. Save the image twice at the end – once with layers open, the other flattened with another name, as a flattened image won't allow you to adjust any stage of your work.

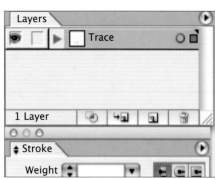

1 Scan an HB pencil sketch which you will use as a guide for vector drawing. Import it into Illustrator and reduce the file size to 100dpi ready to make an accurate Illustrator line trace (the resolution does not need to be large for tracing). Label the layer 'Trace'. If the scan is too dark click on it, then type 50% in the 'Opacity' box.

2 Now create a 'Line' layer and trace the outline of the sketch using the Pen tool, ensuring you click on the 'no fill' box. Give the Pen tool a 2pt stroke. Give the line extra weighting by clicking on the drawing and selecting Expand (Object > Expand), then use the Direct Selection tool to drag out anchor points to thicken the line in selected areas.

3 Lock the 'Line' layer and then create a new 'Flat colour' layer below it. Choose the hues you want from the palette. Colour the different parts of your cartoon figure by selecting within the vector drawn points, leaving the background for a later stage. Use smaller brushes for small areas, and the 'Bucket Fill' tool for filling large shapes.

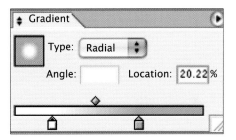

4 Create another new layer and call it 'Shading'. Darken the colours you are going to use for shading by adding 15% black to each one. Draw in the shadow areas and fill these shapes with a colour block from the selected palette; click on more colours in the palette for a more extensive range. Remember to lock the 'Flat' colour layer before you begin.

5 The pattern on the bathing shorts is composed of simple flower shapes. Create a single shape and locate it in the symbols library. Select it using the Sprayer tool and it will spray multiple flowers across the shorts area. Use the Direction Selection tool to remove stray flowers or rearrange the pattern. Create the gradated circle highlight on the rubber ring by selecting the white colour, clicking on the Gradient (next to layers) and selecting 'Radial'. Move the slider bars to adjust the size.

6 Make another layer and create the waves. Outline their shapes and add movement strokes (above). Select a brush from the Artistic Ink range (click on brushes arrow in the palette, scroll down to Open Brush Library > Artistic Ink > select Brush) and fill the areas with blue (right). Add colour gradients to the sea and sky on this layer: select an area with the Marquee tool or Magic Wand and click the Gradient tool to fill the area with the default gradient; black fading to white. The Gradient palette allows you to edit the colours and the 'gradient stops' (where a colour blends into another). To change the gradient's direction, draw a line with the Gradient tool across a previously selected gradient. Return to the Line layer and outline the seagulls, the strokes behind the surfboard and the foam bubbles.

Combining programs

Moving between programs provides more opportunity for creative image play. For example, a standard vector-drawn cartoon character imported into a bitmap program, such as Photoshop, can inhabit surroundings created in an array of styles, from the photographic to the painterly. This freedom to juxtapose the usual and the unusual and bring about striking contrasts invariably unleashes new levels of creativity.

The fact that Photoshop and Illustrator are complementary Adobe stablemates is liberating. The two applications share enough similarities of style and usage for anyone familiar with one application to switch between the two without difficulty. Following this lead, software packages from other manufacturers, such as the Corel Painter program, are deliberately intended to be similar.

Practice exercise: Combining Illustrator and Photoshop

It is important to explore the potential offered by marrying vector and bitmap systems with a wide-open mind. Let go of all expectations of digital precision in favour of more relaxed collisions of broad shapes and colours. Unlike conventional drawing and painting, the Photoshop (bitmap) painting being on a layer can 'go over' the line that you have drawn in Illustrator (vector). When the colouring layer is physically placed beneath the line (vector) layer and the layer 'eye' icons clicked on, it is an easy task to erase colour that has extended over the lines.

Such freeform digital images show that computer-generated concepts can be as inventive as traditional mixed-media collage. There is a benefit too of easily moving layers on top of each other with no need for using glue, which makes it hard to remove the pictorial pieces.

2 Find a photograph of pumpkins or other fruit or vegetables. This can be sourced from the Internet, a magazine or it could be a photo you have taken on a digital camera. Scan or import the picture into Photoshop where it automatically becomes a new 'Photos' layer. Position and scale the picture to the size you want using the Transform tool (Edit > Transform > Scale), and remove unwanted areas with a soft Eraser tool.

Tip: Don't think too long and hard about how you will develop an idea before testing it on screen. Start your exploratory journey straightaway, knowing that any wrong turns are easily corrected or eradicated if they have been made on separate layers.

1 Draw the figure outline in Illustrator, using the Pen tool with a 0.5pt stroke. Label this layer 'Line' and lock it. Now make a new layer named 'Colour' and fill the outline with the different shades seen here. When you are happy with your image, save it for safekeeping, and open Photoshop. In Illustrator, click on 'Select All' to collate all image layers, and drag the picture into your new Photoshop window. Alternatively, you can import the picture by dragging your Illustrator document from your folder or desktop on to the Photoshop icon, where it will open automatically as a new layer in the layers palette.

3 Import the animal pictures into the Photos layer, position them and erase any extraneous details. Create the background layer and sit it below the others. Outline the tree and the amorphous shape behind the figure using the Pen tool. Fill them with gradated colour blends.

4 Distort the blend within the tree shape using the Smudge tool and add digital images of apples as a new layer above the rest. On another layer add a shadow beneath the pumpkins using a soft brush. This gives them extra realism and enhances the 3-D quality. You could refine the shadow using filters.

Composite variation

Blending Illustrator and Photoshop applications can produce great results and they are not too difficult to grasp with a little practice. The hardest challenge lies in creating the initial sketch and controlling the tools for the best effect.

City man ▶
A sketch is created in Illustrator using Brush tools, which give a fluid line of varying thickness. The colour is then filled in and the image dragged into a new Photoshop document which contains layers of scanned magazine pictures with adjusted hues. Applying filters adds drama to the background.

Composite programs caricature

Illustrator is the best choice for creating the extended lines and curves in this composition. The stylized shapes of the body, guitar, amp and microphone are tinted using flat Illustrator colours. The brushed acrylic layers of the more realistic caricatured head are produced in Photoshop.

Guitar man ▼
The flatness of the Illustrator body is in direct contrast with the formed, more painterly textures of the Photoshop head. This has been pinched, tweaked and distorted using an array of brushes and filters.

Digital faces

Speech bubbles are rarely the first point of contact in a visual story and can even be replaced in a dialogue scene by the facial expressions of the characters. It is essential to portray expressions so that they are instantly recognizable, or else risk losing the meaning or joke they are aiming to convey. You can avoid this by reminding yourself that a digital program is only a tool and continue the habit of observing and sketching a range of faces and expressions to keep your skills intact. A portrait that is built using conventional methods can be ruined if something goes wrong at an advanced stage. The advantage of developing a portrait on the screen is that it is almost impossible to go wrong – you just erase the work on the layer and start all over again. The exercises below outline the strikingly different results that can be produced when using different programs to draw faces.

Practice exercise: Using Bezier curves and flat colour in Illustrator

Illustrator is ideal for creating strong controlled lines thanks to the sharp precision of its Bezier curves. While the colouring style limits itself to fairly flat hues, these are perfect for those cartoons where bold graphic definition is necessary. Cartoon artwork produced for television and web pages especially benefits from this flat saturated colour style because they are transmitted by light passing through a dense network of tiny dots.

Tip: Practise the exercises on these pages again but change the brush shapes and sizes, alter the effects used and, in the case of Painter, try out different media or different combinations.

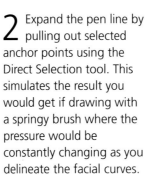

4 Create the final layer to include the shadows and highlights, which are fairly simple. The lighting effect on the top of the hair is made by reducing Opacity and by softening using the Blending tool. The highlight tones on the skin are created by reducing the percentage value of the colour saturation. The shadow on the left has an extra 15% of black added. Take care not to overdo the contrasts on these effects as this could overwhelm the line/colour style of the cartoon.

1 Scan in your pencil sketch at a high resolution and then resample it at 100dpi. Draw over all the lines of this image using the Pen tool. Make the pen drawing into a 'Line' layer and knock back the layer Opacity to 50%. This enables the new image to stand out from the original sketch beneath which was used as a guide.

2 Expand the pen line by pulling out selected anchor points using the Direct Selection tool. This simulates the result you would get if drawing with a springy brush where the pressure would be constantly changing as you delineate the facial curves.

3 Establish a 'Flat Colour' layer and position it below the Line layer in the layers palette. Colour the main areas using a flesh tone for the skin and brown for the hair, beard, eyes and eyebrows. Outline a new shape for the zigzagging edge of the beard.

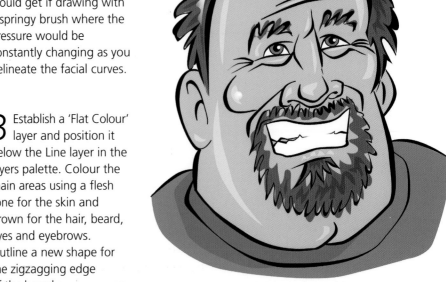

Practice exercise: Modelling in Painter

The tactile joy of painting need not be totally lost for the digital cartoonist. The methodology for building and refining a character portrait through stages of modelling can be successfully employed using the bitmap program Painter. The stylus is sensitive and can take a bit of getting used to, but its readiness to respond to the slightest alteration of hand pressure is a real plus point, and will result in the subtleties which bring a painting to life being retained.

1 Scan in your pencil trace for the base layer. On a new layer, block in the 'Acrylic' colours using broad strokes on a medium brush setting.

2 Smooth the colours using the Blending tool, using the same stroke directions that you would if you were actually painting. Add highlights and smooth them with the same tool. Dash in the T-shirt colour and smooth, first the blue, then the white, then blend. Use a smaller brush to detail the eyes and hair.

Practice exercise: Balancing line with tone in Photoshop

The versatility of Photoshop can be fully realized in this exercise, in which it is used to construct the same face. A quick comparison shows that this Photoshop version creates a happy medium. The lines are crisp yet maintain much of the freely drawn nature of the original pencil sketch. The depth of colour and modelling is convincing enough to add form to the character without making it appear heavily laboured. The evenness of the tonal passages echoes the controlled manual application of gouache or acrylic.

3 Create another layer for shading. Darken the flesh tone by adding a further 15% of black. Darken the hair colour by at least 20% and locate shadows below the hairline and down the right side of his face. Create a gradated blend for the T-shirt on the same layer, extending it from white to blue. Return to the 'Skin' layer and remove the colour on the teeth with the Eraser tool, making them bright white.

1 Scan your pencil sketch in grayscale at 600dpi, reduce it to 300dpi and convert to RGB colour. Under Image > Adjustments > Hue/Saturation move the slider so that the pencil line changes to warm brown. Make a new 'Skin' layer and place it beneath the Line layer. Use the Sprayer tool to apply a gradated skin tone, carefully erasing any excess.

2 Add a new layer between Line and Skin and use a flat brush to paint in warm brown strokes for the beard and hair. Select the same hue to paint in the pupils of the eyes. It is important to use different types and sizes of brush for the various sections of this painting. Opting for one or two choices will limit the contrasts you are aiming for.

Digital face styles

The versatility of computer-generated cartoon faces is seen below. Paint and draw programs are capable of creating styles as wide-ranging as those produced by traditional methods. It makes sense to take inspiration from the master cartoonists when developing a look, whether square-jawed Hanna-Barbera or wide-eyed manga. Clarity of expression and good definition are essential to whatever style you create, and digital media delivers this.

PHOTOSHOP

Sketch ▲
A lively pencil sketch is coloured brown in Photoshop, then a new layer overpainted for a flattish surface form.

Highlighted ▲
A Photoshop image drawn on screen. The ultra-pale highlights and strokes are made with a 1-pixel brush.

Airbrush ▲
A line sketch is scanned and coloured in Photoshop on a new layer. Airbrush Eraser creates highlights on the face.

Flat tones ▲
A Photoshop creation executed with the broken line of a Brush tool and painted in flat hues.

ILLUSTRATOR

Highlighted ▲
The entire face is created in Illustrator with point-created shapes, expanded lines and white highlight strokes.

Gradated tint ▲
The lines are expanded in Illustrator by pulling anchor points. The gradated tint is created on a new layer.

Conventional ▲
An Illustrator drawing that uses Bezier curves throughout, expanded line and layers of flat colour.

Strong shapes ▲
The strong flat-coloured shapes of this face make the most of Illustrator's Bezier curves.

COMBINED

Painter layers ▲
The face was drawn and filled in Illustrator, then imported into Photoshop where a halftone pattern was added.

Broad line ▲
This face fully utilizes expanded Illustrator lines and dots. The pale hair is Photoshop-created.

Line and airbrush ▲
An expanded Illustrator outline that has been coloured in Photoshop. The stubble is airbrushed.

Soft brush and airbrush ▲
The Illustrator outline is coloured in Photoshop. A soft brush defines the hair and the stubble is airbrushed.

Photoshop hair effects

Like faces, distinctive hair styles can be a useful way of defining character and displaying personality traits that are easy to recognize. Exploring the wide range of custom brushes and filter effects in Photoshop and applying them to simple sketches will enable you to spend less time creating techniques, and discover more ways of bringing hair to life. The simple sketches on this page demonstrate some of the effects that can be achieved.

Stage 1 ▲
A pen sketch is scanned and imported into Photoshop. The first duplicate layer is filled with flat medium brown.

Stage 2 ▲
On a new layer the Pencil tool defines hair strands and darker brown brushstrokes soften the edges.

Stage 3 ▲
White highlights are added on the final layer with a medium brush and blended with the Smudge tool at 60% Opacity.

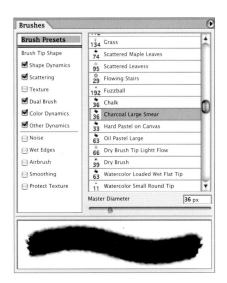

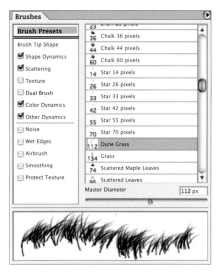

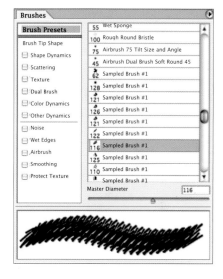

Soft volume ▲
With the charcoal brush selected (Brush Palettes > Brushes), broadly sketch the soft curls. Offer a more life-like balance of tones throughout by altering the 'Opacity', which here is 60% and 30%.

Dune Grass custom brush ▲
Use the custom brush 112 – 'Dune Grass' – from the brushes library to recreate a thinning wispy head of hair. To tidy, use the Eraser tool to remove unwanted strands.

Sampled brush ▲
The variety of custom brushes is wide, the choices peculiar, but they bring strong textural qualities to the drawing in contrast to the flatness of outline and solid, facial colour.

Creating backgrounds

The importance of backgrounds in anchoring cartoon figures, setting scenes and generally assisting the narrative of a gag or strip is undeniable. Creating settings by hand can be laborious but a task such as painting a soft gradated blend or cross-hatching a texture is achieved quickly and easily using digital techniques. Not only is it possible to add uncomplicated backgrounds in seconds, they can be constructed in multiple layers to give you the option of changing textures, colours or line work at will. The freedom of creating settings digitally also allows you to be more inventive in areas such as tonal contrast and surface quality, which can add significant interest to your scenes. Take inspiration from the digitally devised settings of many graphic novels and children's books and don't be afraid to indulge in creative play. Photoshop's wide selection of filters and effects can make for a polished end result, whereas Painter is best able to mimic traditional painterly effects.

Practice exercise: Creating a background in Photoshop

It is especially easy to create, manipulate or duplicate images or sections of images using Photoshop. The typical 'copy and paste' method can be used to build a background, where manual methods would need to employ collage techniques to achieve the same results. As well as its compatibility with other programs, a major benefit of Photoshop is that colours are altered with ease and layers are stacked on top of each other with varying degrees of Opacity.

Tip: Photoshop and Painter have a huge range of filters and effects. Search through these before you create a new texture – the effect you seek may already exist.

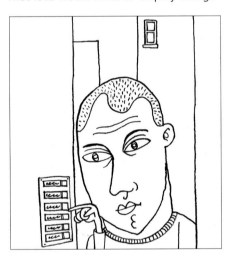

1 Draw the outline using a dip pen and black Indian ink (the single window is deliberate) and scan it into a new Photoshop document. Duplicate it as a layer and rename it 'Line'. Set the layers box on to 'Mutiply'.

4 ▲ ▶ Scale the pattern as you did for the window in step 2 and apply it to the buildings receding into the distance. When the buildings are covered, erase the pattern over the windows.

2 Lasso or Marquee the single window with the appropriate tool and duplicate (Item > Step and repeat) on a new layer. Create the distant windows by scaling (Edit > Transform > Scale), and duplicating the single window. Play around, moving and scaling the shapes until you get the sense of depth you want.

3 Make a new layer and create a brick pattern on it by drawing boxes and fill with two reddish tones. To duplicate the boxes, take them into pattern mode (Edit > Fill > Pattern).

5 Create a new layer to go behind the bricks. Fill it with gradated colour from pale yellow to glowing orange-red and add pale block shapes to indicate the far distance. Fill the bell pushes with red and tint the figure a blue shade that contrasts with the glowing eyes. Draw and fill a darker shadow on a new layer.

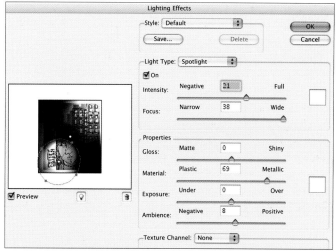

6 Finally enhance the mood using the Lighting Effects palette (Filter > Render > Lighting Effects). Select the values shown in the screengrab above for the light around the bell push. You can adjust the circumference, shape and position of the flare by clicking on the lamp icon and dragging the Pointer tool. Feel free to experiment with new values to discover different effects.

Painter backgrounds

The subtle colours, textures and geometry of this background setting for a tree-planting 'eco-hero' character is created in Painter. This program comes closest to reproducing traditional drawn and painted effects, while Photoshop's range of filters and effects can produce a slicker, more polished look.

Rainbow ◄
To make the rainbow, a series of vertical bands is drawn on a new layer and filled with a spectrum of colours. The colours are then blurred by applying a filter. The bands are distorted and rotated to imitate the rainbow curve. This layer is placed on top of the pastel one.

The figure ▼
The last step is to detail the figure. The scanned image is outlined in broken-edged pencil and filled with colour – acrylic paint tones for the costume and skin, with white chalk pastel highlights. The clouds and rain streaks are pastel, and blocks of grey and brown acrylic tones are duplicated on to a grey background for the buildings.

Scan and pastel effects ▲
A pencil sketch of the superhero and the background details is imported into Painter from the scan application and converted into a layer. The sky is a construction of blues and violets using broad brush tools on a pastel setting. The larger shapes are duplicated and overlapped.

Practice exercise: 3-D illusion in Illustrator

Not every cartoon background works as a simple tone or texture, or a figment of the artist's imagination. For certain subjects it is often necessary to opt for a more lifelike 3-D setting. Converting a flat surface pattern to one which converges at a vanishing point can be a time-consuming exercise by traditional methods but is a relatively problem-free task on the computer. The accuracy of Illustrator makes it the ideal tool for making such drawings. However, their success or failure will depend on the user's grasp of the principles of perspective. A sound understanding, plus the ability to combine different elements convincingly, will enable you to be ambitious in your creations.

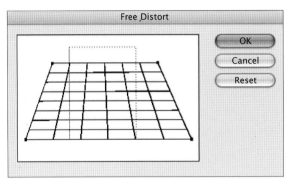

3 ▼ Use the Bucket-Fill tool to colour the squares in a chequerboard pattern. Click the box marked 'Gradient' on the desktop to apply a gradated tint to the colour as shown below. This will greatly enhance the 3-D effect.

2 Lay the grid in perspective along a horizonal plane using Free Distort. Click and move the two end points of the top horizontal line closer together. Adjust their positions until the shape is at the correct perspective. Click 'Reset' if you want to begin again.

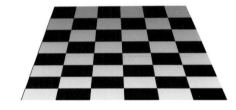

1 On your base layer, start by making the grid pattern for the floor. Use the Pen tool to draw small squares – duplicate one six times to make a row, using the 'Copy and Paste' commands, then duplicate the row eight times to make your grid. Arrange the rows as shown above. Make sure you apply an outline stroke to the grid. Select and group the composite parts of the grid into a single entity (Object > Group).

4 Create a new layer for the dog and food bowls. Position the dog in the midground and the bowls in the foreground. Draw their outlines using the Brush tool, expanding and thickening the lines to add character. Colour the body grey, then select Effect > Stylize > Scribble for a textured look.

5 Select, duplicate and scale the food bowls at different sizes on a new layer. Locate them in the foreground, midground and background. Make a 'Shadows' layer beneath the bowls, outline an ellipse and fill it with grey at 50% Opacity. Duplicate, scale and position the shadows beside the bowls.

Tip: Keep perspective grids simple so that you are able to judge the perspective convergence easily. Refer to one, two and three perspective template drawings to help you to understand how settings and objects converge into the distance.

Practice exercise: Stylish realism using combined programs

A modern setting needs a style to match. Amalgamating the accuracy of Illustrator and the versatility of Photoshop gives you the means to produce an image with a bold and contemporary look. The broadly painted background of this setting is made in Photoshop while the Illustrator line, strong graphic shapes and accurate perspective refine the picture and add realism. The creative process of laying down colours, textures and marks in distinctive layers is as involved as the traditional technique of screenprinting.

1 The room and its contents are outlined in Illustrator using a range of brushes to give a free loose style. The flat colour is applied in Illustrator and the series of dots for shadow areas on the lemons is created using the Blend tool.

2 The image is then dragged into Photoshop where the colours are adjusted and the larger areas filled with broad brushstrokes. A refined Brush tool is employed to create the smooth lines of the MP3 player.

Tip: Adding scanned or 'found' imagery to your hand-drawn compositions, as with the iPod above, can grant them greater legitimacy than as images alone. Think of the photographic trees, people and vehicles used to bring the latest digital architectural renderings to life. Keep a cuttings file of useful photographs or magazine clips that could be scanned and cut out digitally using Photoshop. Collect subjects that have a strong shape and not too much tonal subtlety.

3 Finally, a 'Halftone' filter creates a border. A regular coarse pattern of halftone dots can be applied in Photoshop to interrupt the smooth surface of Illustrator-generated images. The settings used here are shown on the right. Adjusting dot size, shape and contrast will give different effects.

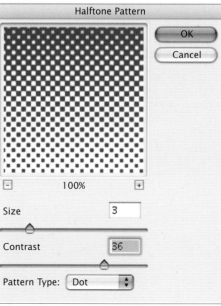

Portraying motion

The computer counterparts of drawn action lines have much in common with the speed effects seen in fast-action photography and film. All the main vector and bitmap programs can replicate the effects of suspending a high-speed moment in time, often with only a few simple steps. Illustration devices that signify movement can be digitally enhanced using a gamut of action effects and distortion tricks. Features such as blurring, speed lines and superimposing multiple images on top of one another all create a convincing illusion of activity. Short of actually making it move, selecting the right interpretation of your moment of frozen time or mixing manipulated digital photography with your cartoon will be enough to animate your image with energy and dynamism. The exercises below outline the creation of composite pictures that refuse to stay still!

Practice exercise: Creating a speed blur effect

To produce a cartoon with digitally animated qualities requires a good balance of elements. A well-constructed composition is vital: the main focus should be emphatic and its descriptive action lines surrounded by enough white space to take the motion effect. Directing the viewer's eye contributes more to the concept of motion than a host of clever tricks. In this exercise the simple device of a looping motion line provides a visual journey starting at the goldfish bowl at the bottom of the picture and leading to the flying fish at the top. Here, a blur effect on the blades is sufficient to focus the full attention of the viewer on its rapid, whirling motion.

1 Create the static rounded fish in Illustrator, expanding the points of your drawn lines with the Direct Selection tool as in previous exercises. Draw the multiple helicopter blades in a lighter line to help them move.

2 Import this line drawing into a new Photoshop document and create a 'Colour' layer. Add the soft yellows and greens to the body using an Airbrush tool. Fill the rotor blades with flat red and paint white in between.

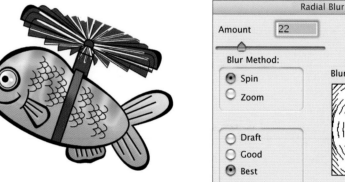

3 Select the elliptical rotor blades area and open the Blur filter (Filter > Blur > Radial Blur), setting the method to spin. Select a second tighter elliptical section in the centre of the same area and repeat the process.

4 Draw the goldfish bowl, the action strokes and twisting line which traces the motion path in Illustrator. On a new layer, position the earlier Illustrator outline of the fish. 'Select All' and open in Photoshop for colouring, positioning the outline beneath the existing colour layer.

Practice exercise: Creating a superimposed effect

Creating the sense of movement in a still image by superimposing is traditionally done using clear acetate layers. The same image is duplicated on each layer, each time in a slightly different position to give the effect of

movement trapped in freeze-frame. Creating this type of action in Photoshop offers the advantage of varying the Opacity of the layers, which allows the transition of time to be more strongly conveyed.

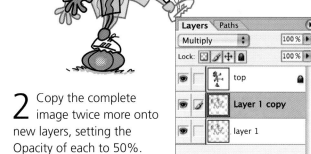

1 Sketch the outline of the boy and his football in pen and scan it in as an oversized line art image. Reduce it in scale and size to 300 dpi, convert it to RGB colour and copy to a new layer. On separate layers, add flat colour, shadows on the left side and a white highlight to the ball.

2 Copy the complete image twice more onto new layers, setting the Opacity of each to 50%. Drag the three layers into a new document and position so that the lower two are slightly offset. Rotate the lower images (Edit > Transform > Rotate) and erase any area overlaps.

3 Finally, add the radial blur motion effect from the Blur filter to the two images on the lower layers (Filter > Blur > Radial Blur). Decide on the frequency value for the blur and set it to spin. Feel free to play around with the settings, experimenting with different values, and only click OK when you are completely satisfied with the results.

Practice exercise: Combining media

Combining images that vary in quality is an easy and effective way of portraying speed. In this example a static Illustrator-generated cartoon character is imposed on a digital photograph which has been 'speeded' up.

1 Choose a digital photograph with a strong one- or two-point perspective, such as the advancing train used here. Import it into Photoshop as a .jpg, then convert it to RGB colour mode (Image > Mode > RGB Colour). Make the photo a new background layer.

2 The outline of the cartoon character is created in Illustrator and imported into Photoshop. The flat colours and highlights are added on a new layer. The speed effect is applied to the digital photo on a new layer using the Radial Blur filter set to 'Zoom'. The layered cartoon is then imported. Finally, an elliptical shadow is drawn in Photoshop and softened using 'feather' at 20 pixels. It is then filled with blue and reduced to 50% Opacity.

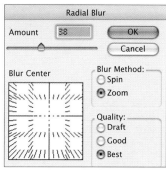

Digital improving

One of the fantastic things about computer enhancement is that it does just as it says: enhance! Each picture that is drawn, painted or manipulated in some way is bound to be an 'okay' picture, but getting it to the next level and making it a little more special can be a really simple task that merely requires you to have the tricks of the trade to hand. Every day that you use graphic applications on a computer your learning will

progress and, second to picking up tips from other people, there is a strong argument for exploring and experimenting with the program's filters and effects libraries. Many of the improvements that will transform your cartoons are achieved by making simple adjustments to one of the wide range of filters or via the Image > Adjustment menu in Photoshop. The preview option always allows you to test the effect.

Practice exercise: Retro style

A return to the retro styles of the 1970s brought with it a desire by image-makers to take another look at the grooviness of swirling patterns, modish pop art circles, tangerine dreams and lime-green walls. Although the colours of the revival are more refined, the defining feature of this retro style remains in its clean lines and strong colour definition. Such specific demands are most successfully met by a combination of Illustrator and Photoshop.

1 Begin with a manual pen drawing that has plenty of life in its line variation. The focus of the sketch is on the listener in the chair with his accessories so keep the background plain. Import this image into Photoshop and tint it using a Colour palette and Brush tools.

2 Construct the rest of the room in Illustrator using the Pen tool. Place the coloured figure into Illustrator at the same time to assist with the scale and construction of the room. Drag everything back into a new Photoshop document. Draw an irregular shape on a new layer beneath the line drawing and colour it green. Draw a box with the Rectangle Drawing tool. 'Posterize' a scanned or downloaded tower-block picture (Layer > New Adjustment Layer > Posterize) and import into the box.

3 Create the swirling wallpaper pattern in Illustrator, and place it back into Photoshop for duplication as a pattern (Filter > Pattern Maker). Select the background area above the skirting boards, and darken it using the histogram slide (Image > Adjustment > Levels). Next choose 'Multiply' on layers, and fill your selection with your chosen pattern (using the Pattern Bucket tool). This will duplicate the pattern into the space.

Practice exercise: Motion in Photoshop

Adding an airbrush-style motion effect is a very uncomplicated process in Photoshop. It is made using basic brushes and any of the blur filters, grain filters or pointillizing filters, singly or combined. The end result can enhance a simple visual gag enormously. In this practice exercise, it can be clearly seen that the definition of contrast between the crisp characterful line and the soft out-of-focus background lends a heightened sense of depth to the final image.

Tip: Using noise, grain and pointillism filters is a quick alternative to sourcing real-world textures to use in your imagery. They have the added bonus of meshing and integrating more naturally with your art.

1 Sketch the 'dog and man' gag by hand as a simple, fineliner pen drawing. Keep your lines lively by varying their weight – it keeps them animated. Scan your drawing and import it into Photoshop, duplicate it as a new layer, delete the background layer and set it to Multiply.

2 Add colour using soft brushes and create the background as a Gradient image (Layer > New Fill Layer > Gradient (set to Multiply)), from light to dark. Further soften the soft coloured banding of the sky and accentuate the effect of motion using the Blur filter (Filter > Blur).

3 Fine action lines deliver effective motion. Add a Horizontal Grain filter (Filter > Grain) to the back of the dog's body. Check the settings against the screengrab (right), but feel free to experiment with intensity and contrast. When you are satisfied click OK.

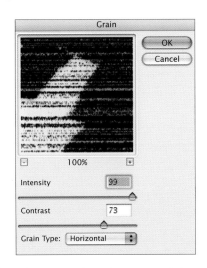

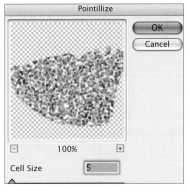

4 Extra details can really enhance the character of a drawing. Marquee/Lasso the jumper area (Select > Filter > Pointillize), set the cell size and click OK. Adding texture to the man's jumper brings him into focus as a foil to the leading character of the pooch.

5 Finally, add white speed lines around the feet of the characters and in between them.

Words

A cartoon with a strong visual sense won't need the help of text to communicate its message. Despite this, words traditionally accompany many cartoons and perform a variety of functions. In general, self-contained panel cartoons have a simple caption or one-liner beneath them, whereas comic strips include dialogue placed inside speech bubbles. Lettering is also used as a means of communicating sound effects.

Cartoon words must be clear, legible and integrate with the overall design. Lettering style, size, weight and consistency are therefore important considerations. Traditionally, cartoonists use hand-drawn lettering to achieve this, a technique that is easily replicated using selected computer fonts. Unless it is being used for emphasis, cartoon lettering is usually black on white so that it plays a secondary role to the image.

Speech bubbles

Digital software is of huge assistance to the cartoonist where accuracy and neatness are essential. A vector drawing program, such as Illustrator, can produce a range of faultless speech-bubble ellipses. Once created, they can be saved into a file and used as a style library for ready access as and when they are needed.

Calligraphic bubbles ▼
Select different brush-drawn styles in Illustrator to produce quirky speech bubbles with varying weights of line. Go to brush style under 'Brushes' and choose the style. Next select the bubble, add the stroke weight of your choice and click on it.

◄ ▼ Basic bubble process
The basic construction of speech bubbles is best done in Illustrator. Draw an ellipse with the Ellipse tool, and then use the Pen tool to make a small inverted triangle at the base of the oval. Go to View > Pathfinder > Make compound shape to unite these two selections.

Only use bold and bold italic where it most **effectively** expresses the idea.

Italic bold can alter pace or *intonation* in speech.

Offer **emphasis** to speech by simply setting in bold**.**

For speech to have strong impact within the narrative, set it all in bold or bold italic.

Plain speaking in a standard, plain bubble

This pressure-led bubble indicates movement and life.

A more basic bubble, in a broken drawn style, is suitable for lighter gags.

Place informal lively speech in a direct, square box-type bubble.

Brush style palette

Pen and Pencil tools

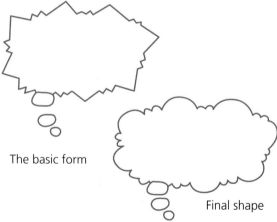

The basic form

Final shape

A thought cloud ▲
Construct the basic form in straight-edged lines using the Pen tool. Then curve the points by adding and subtracting points within the shape, using the range of either Pen or Pencil tools.

Lettering effects

Whether they are vector-drawn or bitmapped, all type forms can be manipulated – stretched, compressed, enlarged, reduced or skewed – and tinted by building layers. Both Illustrator and Photoshop offer a broad range of effects which are useful when you want to exaggerate or emphasize lettering. Effects such as a blended or gradient fill, drop shadow or other tinted or textured surfaces are the most commonly used. If you start to explore the Filter menus you will find not only alternatives for toning and texturing the letters, but also distorting them.

Back Fill

Outline, no fill

Drop Shadow

Drop Shadow
(layer effects)

Chisel Emboss
(layer effects)

Custom Brush
(wavy line fill)

Distorted

Radial Fill

Twist, blend

Duplicated X
offset to new layer

Custom Brush
(advanced palette)

Halftone Pattern
(partially erased)

Special FX in Illustrator ▲
Although Illustrator does not offer the same breadth of tools for manipulation as Photoshop, it is a very good program for adjusting type forms.

Special FX in Photoshop ▲
The above examples show the variability of type effects that are available in Photoshop. The majority show the results that can be achieved by manipulating surface decoration.

Expressive type in Illustrator ▲ ▶
When you have typed the word in your chosen font go to Type > Create Outlines; then Object > Ungroup and use the Direct Selection tool (white arrow) with Alt key depressed to overlap the type. Next go to Filter > Distort > Free Distort and extend the points outwards to alter the scale and shape of the typeface. Finally, apply a Gradient Fill from the gradients palette on your desktop.

Transforming type ▼
The dullest of lettering can be given a visually exciting make-over by manipulating it. Explore the different effects that Illustrator has to offer and experiment with already familiar techniques, such as varying and expanding line widths.

Digital shortcuts

Achieving a complex visual effect using traditional manual methods requires skill, patience and time. When working on a computer the critical difference is that you can gain maximum effects with minimum effort, often after a single keystroke.

Understanding and implementing digital shortcuts to create effects such as the complexities of reflections in glass or on water, or the subtle folds of fabric are indispensable skills for the digital image-maker. Begin by exploring and experimenting with the range of different filters that are at your disposal. Each filter has an accompanying tool option panel which allows you to apply effects and distortions. For example, in the case of the Bas Relief filter, it includes surface texture choices and the depth of the relief dictated by the direction of the light creating the 3-D effect.

Practice exercise: Creating a fabric fold

This exercise demonstrates a digital approach to suggesting the smooth undulating movement of a weightless, shimmering fabric by replicating the complex interplay of light and shade on the surface of the cartoon character's cloak and pantaloons. The huge range of effects and filters that are available in Photoshop makes it the ideal choice of program to achieve such a high standard of description easily, quickly and effectively.

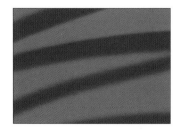 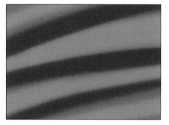 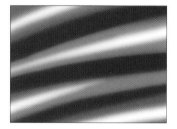 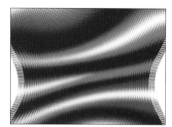

1 For the cloak create a rectangle in Photoshop at the approximate size you need and fill it with red. Add broad, horizontal bands of light brown using a selection of soft brushstrokes to give a streaked effect.

2 Lock the first layer and make a new one. Select a lighter shade of red and brush it across the red areas, ensuring you leave narrow bands of the deeper colour to establish a consistent tonal depth and rhythm.

3 Make another layer and select a smaller soft brush to add tapering white highlights across the centre of each paler colour band. Don't worry about precision. No two fabric folds are ever the same.

4 Now for the digital trickery: go to the Wave filter (Filter > Distort > Wave) and experiment by moving the slidebars until you achieve the desired effect. Click OK when you are happy with the result.

5 To achieve further distortion which is less regular and looks more like silken folds, apply the Pinch filter (Filter > Distort > Pinch) and adjust the level of distortion by moving the slider along the bar. Form the flowing cloak shape by cutting it out using the Pen tool.

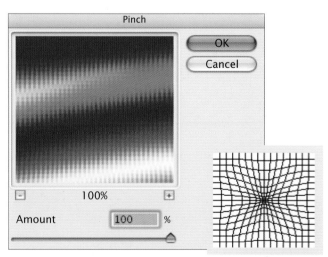

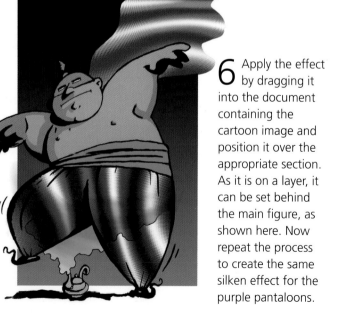

6 Apply the effect by dragging it into the document containing the cartoon image and position it over the appropriate section. As it is on a layer, it can be set behind the main figure, as shown here. Now repeat the process to create the same silken effect for the purple pantaloons.

Practice exercise: Rendering embossed metal

In this example the embossed bronze sheen is created by applying a filter known as Bas Relief. Note that filters can never be a shortcut for working through the creative process and that final effects should only be applied to finished artwork.

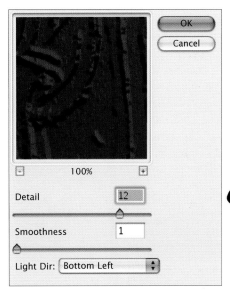

1 Scan the line drawing of the Roman warrior into Photoshop. A new layer is created and placed below the line layer. Flat colour and simple shading are added to bring the character to life.

2 Select the area in question using the Lasso or Marquee selection tool and apply the Bas Relief filter (Filter > Sketch > Bas Relief). It imparts a kind of solarizing effect to the colours and gives a raised appearance to contrasting areas. Set the light direction, level of detail and smoothness you want by operating the sliders.

3 When you have achieved the filter effect, you can apply small finishing touches. Here, a subtle shadow tinted in soft pale green is centred beneath the figure to prevent him from 'floating'.

Practice exercise: Reflections in water

To replicate the reflection in water of an object or figure by hand requires a huge amount of visual understanding and time. Computer drawing programs contain filters designed to produce the effect automatically, releasing you from a very painful learning process. If such an option had been available, the Great Masters might have plumped for it too!

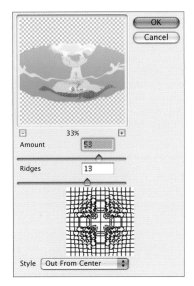

1 Draw the diver freehand in Illustrator and bring into Photoshop on a new layer, where he is reduced in size to fit the area of pool reflection. Apply the Distortion filter and adjust to the required percentage.

2 To add the water surface shimmer, reset the Blending Opacity to 'Hardlight' in Edit > Fill, to give the reflection the correct level of shine. Other options are Filter > Liquefy or Filter > Distort > Glass.

Practice exercise: Creating a mirror image

Achieving a realistic reproduction of a reflected mirror-image is a relatively simple task in the hands of the digital cartoonist. It can be made to look even more convincing with added enhancements, such as reflected light, distortion and reduction. The artists should still rely on their knowledge of how reflection and distortion actually look when seeking to replicate the visual outcome. Reference photographs can help, especially if your subject is moving.

Tip: Use the Ripple filter to distort reflections. Note the differences between a reflection in a moving surface, such as water, and a solid surface, such as glass.

1 Make a pen drawing of the cartoon, scan and import it into Photoshop. Colour it using multiple layers. Create the soft-edged flooring by feathering it (Select > Feather > Feather Radius > 15 pixels). Leave the mirror blank at this stage as you will create the reflection in three stages.

2 Next return to the scanned cowboy. Reverse his image using Image > Rotate Canvas > Flip Canvas Horizontal. Apply the Transform tool (Edit > Transform > Distort) and pull the points of the rectangle around the figure to distort it. Place the reversed image inside the mirror frame.

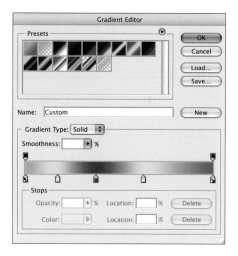

3 Go to the Gradient Editor and set the gradated blue tint for the surface of the mirror. Play with the settings until you achieve the result you want. Apply the effect to the mirror on a new layer that is set to Multiply. This overlays the mirror effect on to your reversed cowboy image.

4 Finally, make the mirrored reflection look more realistic by softening the image so that it appears slightly blurred. To achieve this, apply a Linear Blur to the figure, then use the History brush to partially erase it. Select white from the colour palette, decrease the Opacity to 40% and add white highlight streaks across the surface of the mirror.

Practice exercise: Adding texture with filters

The array of filters available in Photoshop enables you to add various atmospheric effects to your cartoons. A playful attitude is likely to achieve interesting results, so see what happens when you apply a particular filter effect to a layer or two. Juxtaposing texture filters enriches images, for example. Once you have mastered the ordering of the layers palette it is then just a case of adjusting the image to fit and interpreting the cartoon appropriately.

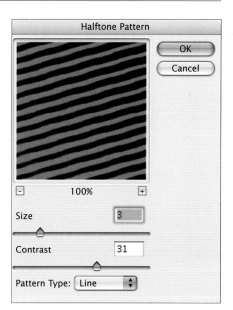

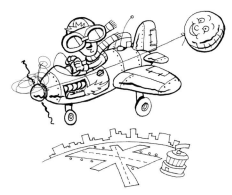

1 Make a line drawing, scan and import it into Photoshop. Duplicate this Background layer and delete the original. This unlocks the copy layer so it is ready to work on.

2 ▲ ▶Use the oval Marquee tool to create an oval shape and soften its painted edge with a Feather (Select > Feather > Feather Radius > 15 pixels). Fill the shape with a blend of blue and pink using the Gradient tool. To do this add a layer of pink to the blue and reduce the Fill and Opacity settings.

3 ▶ Colour the plane by selecting the fuselage section and imposing a Halftone filter on a new layer (Filter > Sketch > Halftone Pattern). Set the filter to Line so that the aircraft body has a lined texture running along its length. Select grey as the tint colour and place this layer above the sky oval.

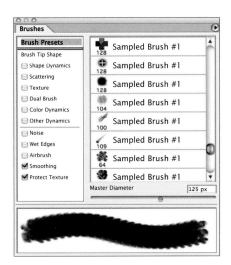

4 ▲ ▶ Erase the filter effect overlapping the sky oval and colour the rest. On separate layers: add a Spin filter to the propeller; select Smoothing and Protect Texture presets for the smoke; blend the flames and clouds with the Smudge tool; and balloon highlights using Filter > Render > Lighting Effects > Flare.

Animation

A sequence of individual pictures that are slightly adjusted as the series progresses can literally come to life before our eyes. According to the Persistence of Vision theory, our brains hold on to each image for a fraction of a second after our eyes have left it. When we see a rapid succession of individual images we think we are witnessing movement. An animated cartoon is a very long series of altering static frames. For the cartoonist who wants to explore this next progression, there are computer animation programs which enable frames to be viewed as a moving sequence. Adobe Flash and ImageReady will provide the beginner with the basic knowledge needed to create moving 2-D cartoons. Those wishing to explore 3-D animation will need software such as 3-D Studio Max or Maya, or cheaper, shareware alternatives available on the Internet. However, depicting a moving figure is a skilful undertaking requiring a keen understanding of animal and human movement.

Basic techniques

The simplest forms of effective animation do not need a movie camera to produce results. A sequence of images, each with a slight alteration, drawn on consecutive pages of a sketchpad results in a moving 'film' when the pages are rapidly flicked. The humble flick book is a commonly used prototype for developing the movements and characteristics of animated characters and a must for cartoonists who want to bring their creations to life. As well as creating action it is also a means of experimenting with the effects of distortion. Exaggerating the natural forces of gravity and motion on characters and objects brings them into the sphere of the humorously absurd. Getting your figures moving around the cartoon world is a powerful trigger for generating new and fresh ideas.

Flick book ▼
The simplest form of drawn animation can be tested by making a flick book. A series of images is sketched on consecutive pages so that each 'traces' over the top of the next. Each new drawing is slightly altered so that the images seem to move when the pages are rapidly flicked. For best results, make sure the pages are flush and evenly cut.

Deformation: bouncing ▼
This sequence illustrates the deformation of a ball as it falls and lands on a flat surface. The distorted shape is most marked at the impact stage, returning to normal as it prepares to bounce up again. The exaggeration of the altered shape is much greater than it would be in reality and the illustration of the process as a frozen moment provides a strong sense of movement. A cartoon animation that did not jump and move would seem static and dull.

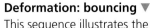

Tracking movement ▲
How you draw a character and the devices you use can lend it strong animated properties. The bee in both pictures has active features: the feelers have eyes, the overlapping wings suggest flight and the vertical body stripes bounce the viewer's eyes from left to right. The dotted trails effectively confirm the direction of the movement.

Deformation: Compression and stretching

The great thing about animating an image is that it does not have to mirror reality. The goal is to create a movement that is believable in the surreal cartoon world where people and objects are malleable and can spring back into shape as if made of rubber. Techniques such as exaggerated compression and elongation are commonly used in cartoon animation to enhance or emphasize a movement, lending the action additional impact and power.

> **Tip:** Devote a number of flick books to deformation, bouncing, compression and elongation. Start with simple line drawings and only add colour and detail when these are working fluidly.

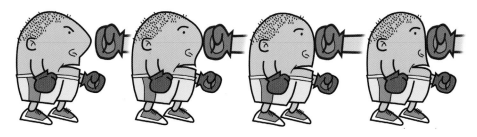

Compression ◄
The repeated images and the depression of the nose on the impact of the glove are essential. The shape and size of the nose gives it all the focus. The fact that the images remain identical serves to enhance the effect of the increasing indent as the nose is punched.

Elongation ◄
The same repetition but this time the boxer's stance steadily becomes more elongated as he ducks away from the second blow. The fighter begins to tilt back in anticipation, before his body stretches out of all proportion as the fist makes its first appearance.

Flash animation program

Flash is a vector-based program that can manipulate vector and bitmap graphic images and also supports audio and video files. It operates a language called ActionScript and as a package enables animations to be created for games, movies and Internet uses, such as online greetings cards, website navigation bars and advertisement banners. The content of Flash documents can be embedded into mobile phones and other portable players too. Files are saved in the SWF format (Shock Wave Flash) and are most commonly played through software known as a Flashplayer.

Flash is being used with more frequency to display video clips on web pages and it has compatibility for both Microsoft and Macintosh operating systems. With its user-friendly menus, tools and its frame-by-frame approach to building the animated sequence, it is relatively simple to use and the perfect beginner's introduction to animation. A running timeline dealing in frames per second helps you to keep track of your work in progress, and you can isolate individual frames or divide them into 'scene' sections and work in layers in much the same way as you would with Photoshop, Painter, Illustrator or Freehand. The key processes of Flash are included in this section to enable you to bring your cartoon creations to life.

Typical Flash window ▲
A toolbar runs down the left-hand side of the document, and the layer icon is to the right of it. The timeline runs across the top and the slider bar can be placed at any point on it to select a specific moment. The drips of the spaceman's lolly between frames will show sequential movement.

Connecting the moving parts

A cartoon animator has a multi-part role: first as inventor of a cast of characters and their narrative; next as image-maker, storyboarding and creating artwork sequences, either manually or digitally. Finally, with the images imported into an animation program, the cartoonist becomes editor/director. The success or failure of the animation, however, depends on how convincingly a character moves within and relates to its setting. Aspiring animators must grasp the connection of the moving parts of a cartoon figure. To achieve this, animators often use starting points which might easily be dismissed as child's play, even when the end product is highly sophisticated. In much the same way as a simple flat card puppet is created out of body parts, so might the animator initially approach the subject of movement in this way.

Construction ▼

This cartoon witch is constructed from a series of simple flat coloured shapes created in Illustrator or Flash. The parts are then built into a figure with a life and character of its own. The freedom to make corrections and changes along the way is part of the process.

Pivot points ▶

The red circles indicate the chief pivot points which will allow the witch to move freely. All animators use these same central points of movement as starting points. In fact, it is traditional practice to construct a jointed card maquette.

Sequential duplication ▶

This duplicated sequence demonstrates the subtle movement achieved by slightly manipulating each of the pivot points. Our senses are attuned to the tiniest changes and very little alteration is needed to communicate a sense of animation. The smaller the change is, the smoother the transition to another position and the more convincing the animation.

Keeping backgrounds simple

Perversely, in animation you do not necessarily have to make the elements physically move to describe it or create its illusion. When the brain realizes the 'jump' in information, carefully planned scaling and placing of objects in a setting can give the effect that the

viewer is in a sense the animator. Since animations tend to be busy, a 'breather' is welcome between frames. Any artist or designer of images should always be thinking of ways to create the illusion of movement with as few flashy effects as possible. A scene with too many

elements can become overfussy, and the viewer may not know where to look. Check out some of the best animations and you will find that the backgrounds are fairly plain and understated with very little movement, allowing the characters to take centre stage.

Movement in space ▶
By increasing or decreasing the scale of both the background and the foreground (the head and shoulders of the girl) it's possible to suggest movement. By moving the girl around the frame and depicting her in a range of different sizes, the illusion of depth is naturally suggested. The simplicity of this concept offers the cartoon a charm – the motion will be jaunty if frames are animated.

Movement and 3-D illusion ▶
Much can be achieved through the use of Illustrator or Photoshop layers. Trickery of scale and positioning gives the images their illusory, moving qualities.

The spaceman enters the screen from the left, where he is fairly large. The trail of the spaceship offers direction to the astronaut – streaking from left in the first image and from the right in the second, where he is considerably smaller, indicating distance.

Simple sequencing

It is vital to plan the narrative of an animated sequence with care. Breaking down the action into single frames that present concise visual information is a key part of the process. Keeping consistency between the frames will offer a believable transition between them.

Key frame 1 *Key frame 2* *Key frame 3*

Key frames ◀
The top row reveals the key frames of the narrative: spotting the fly; catching the fly; and eating the fly. The information is clearly presented and no more than the necessary elements are included in each frame.

――――― *Interim frames* ―――――

More frames ◀
Adding interim frames containing a lesser degree of movement will make the motion appear smoother and less abrupt.

Digital projects

With the technical knowledge in place, you can now apply it to set projects, considering digital caricature, developing the digital collage, creating the graphic novel and cartoon strip and simple, computer animation. This section will get you started as a digital cartoonist and point you in the right direction so that you may develop your own personal vision and interpretation.

Creating caricatures

The cartooning tradition of caricaturing famous people is essentially a hand-drawn process. However, combining traditional and digital skills grants you the opportunity to work up an initial drawing into an image that wholly encapsulates the personality you are portraying. With digital drawing and painting programs, it is easy to correct mistakes, work the same image up with different media and experiment without consequence. You are also able to add background elements and build up vivid colour through easily adjustable layers. The following projects are created using Photoshop and Illustrator programs.

Caricature: Bob Marley

1 Make a loose line drawing in pen and black Indian ink. Overemphasize the head for comic effect. Your aim is to capture the essence of the subject, so be sure to add in iconic props, such as Marley's microphone and Rastafarian hat.

2 Scan the image at 300dpi, then open it in Photoshop. Set up a new layer and set to 'Multiply' mode for the colours. Using a variety of Photoshop's textured brushes with medium (50%) Opacity, build up sketchy, appropriately laid-back areas of colour and shade. Don't worry about fully colouring any of the areas – you don't want your final piece to look too 'finished'.

Final image

This final image is coloured and built using Photoshop. It has been created through the relatively easy process of layers, stacked from the background up. Once the image was essentially in place, Marley's facial features were refined using Photoshop to reshape the eyes, nose, brows and mouth. The changes are subtle, but the result is an image that looks that much more like its subject.

3 Continue with the rest of the face and clothes, gradually adding strokes of different strengths and direction until the subject becomes more solid without losing its lively energetic qualities. Notice that the light direction is from left to right – even when working in a loose, free style try to be aware of this.

4 For the background, make the flag of Marley's beloved Jamaica on a separate layer, sitting beneath all the others. Create three rectangles of flat colour, blurred using the appropriate Filter (Filter > Blur). Erase the white areas on both the Colour and Line Art layers so that the flag shows through – the quickest way to do this is to select the white with the Magic Wand tool (set to 'Contiguous' with around 25 'Tolerance'), then press delete. Clean up stray areas of white with the Eraser tool.

Caricature: Mahatma Gandhi

3 Remove the excess background colour by carefully tracing around the drawn outline with the Eraser tool. Click on the Zoom tool (the magnifying glass icon), to get close-up views of the different areas. This is especially necessary for deleting colour between the fingers, for example. Clicking the mouse will zoom in closer. When the area outside your figure is selected, return to the Colour layer and press delete. This will remove the brown areas outside your linework. Clear up any loose areas of brown with the Eraser tool.

1 Make a simple outline pen drawing of Gandhi referenced from a source using a black fineliner or the equivalent. Here, we draw attention to his modest attire, his famous spectacles and warm, good-natured eyes. The oversized, imbalanced ears add humour.

2 Scan the image and open it in Photoshop. Duplicate the layer, delete the 'Background' layer, and set its options to 'Multiply'. Make a new layer, call it 'Background Colour' and tint a rectangle light brown.

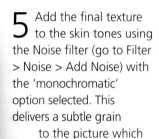

5 Add the final texture to the skin tones using the Noise filter (go to Filter > Noise > Add Noise) with the 'monochromatic' option selected. This delivers a subtle grain to the picture which is then slightly 'formed' using the Emboss filter (Stylize > Emboss). Select a stippling brush for the grey hair. On a new background colour, layer spray-in colour at 50% Opacity, using a soft brush.

4 Create new layers for the shading and highlights. Using a soft brush for each, model the muscles and give definition to the face and body. Create another layer for the white highlight strokes – these are also made using a soft brush. Caricatures tend to benefit from a single, strong light source (here off to the top right of the drawing). At this stage, we have also finished off the eyes and mouth with pupils and teeth drawn in on the flat colour layer. Use a hard, spherical brush for the pupils and white highlights in the eyes.

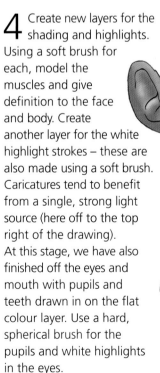

Final image

Gandhi has been created through a definite layer process: First, the bold outline drawing offered a template for filling in with colour and tone. Next, an overall colour on the whole figure became the base on to which soft brush effects and highlights were built in consecutive layers to make him appear more 3-D. A final, softly sprayed background and subtle use of filters offered the image 'polish'.

Caricature: Elvis Presley

3 Select a very large soft brush and draw the hair in black. On a series of new layers (or on the same layer, if you are feeling confident), add a swathe of white on top at a lesser Opacity, so that the black underneath shows through. Use this wash as a base for the vertical white highlight strokes (use a new layer if you need to), which are modelled using a crescent-shaped brush from the brush menu.

1 Use a soft B pencil to sketch and shade the Elvis caricature in head-larger-than-body style. Note how the pose chosen reflects Elvis's 'snakelike hips' in the form of a reverse 'S'. Block in his expanse of characteristic hair, but leave it unshaded for the moment. Scan the drawing and open it in Photoshop. Create a duplicate layer and delete the drawing on the original background one to leave you a layer for colouring. Go to Image > Adjustments > Hue/Saturation and change the pencil line to blue using the sliders.

4 Blur the white highlight strokes and add tints of blue and brown. Finally, re-establish the detailing by adding a few hanging strands of black hair trailing across Elvis's forehead, again on a new layer. Now revisit each layer, adjusting marks or colours as needed. When you are satisfied with the result, go to the Layers > Flatten Image command. Elvis has left the building!

2 Choose a large, coarse brush from the palette, set it to 'Dissolve' and sweep washes of colour on to the new layer crossing the pencil lines. Dissolve creates colours with broken, speckled textures. Select blue from the colour palette for the jeans and yellow for the shirt. Add some blue into the flesh and use the Eraser for highlights.

Final image
Elvis is treated with more traditional use of techniques to match the 1950s' rock 'n' roll years to which this image pertains. The selection of colour palettes, their layered transparency and use of soft, Photoshop brushes have helped to achieve this dated effect, which in turn communicates to the viewer the singer as an icon of his time.

Caricature: Marilyn Monroe

Final image
A line drawing provides a framework for blocks of soft tonal hues which are blended using tools and filters in Illustrator. Shadows and highlights add a strong, graphic quality with clean, contrasting shapes. Equally strong shapes in the facial detailing of the eyes and hair strands offer a crisp, linear and all together sparkly finish!

1 Draw a pencil caricature of Marilyn Monroe. Scan it, then open it in Illustrator. Go to the 'Window' menu, select 'Transparency' and change the Opacity to 90%, so that the pen lines will show up on top of the sketch layer. Create a new layer (Pen Outline) and draw over the scanned outline using a different colour for each area of the portrait – hair, lips, skin.

2 Still in Illustrator, block in the coloured shapes on a new layer or series of layers, placed beneath the Pen Outline. Use complementary tones to the colours used in your outline – the outlines should be the darkest colour, from which you can select warm midtones for most areas. Work up extra detail by filling the brows and adding eye shadow.

3 Soften the hair tone using the Blend tool, carefully stroking the cursor so that the blends follow the direction of the waves. On a new layer create a star shape by manipulating a basic polygon using the 'Free Distort' filter (go to Filter > Free Distort). Finally, add white highlights to the eyes, face and lips to give Marilyn some Hollywood gloss and shine. Suggest a dazzling smile with a broken grey line across the white expanse of teeth.

Painterly style of Photoshop

The sophisticated performance of Adobe Photoshop as a paint program cannot be overestimated. It is the most versatile application available to computer artists and a digital tool that can take a user through the same stages of the artistic process met by a traditional painter. The beauty of this package lies in the relative ease with which mistakes can be rectified. Artists can take a scanned sketch, lay down base tones and transform this into a fully 'painted' image by adding layers of colour in a way that recalls working with acrylics or oils.

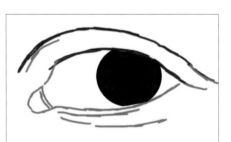

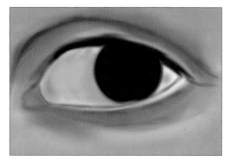

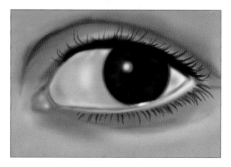

Initial drawing ▲
A painted-style digital image always starts with an outline. Whether this comes from a sketch imported via a scan, or from a series of rough lines laid on the digital canvas with the mouse or drawing tablet, is a question of personal preference.

Building tones ▲
The first stage is to lay down a series of base colours that provide a midground spread of colour on to which you model shadows and highlights. The options in Photoshop allow you to mimic natural media, from oils to acrylics and more.

Final details ▲
Varying Opacities, sizes and hardnesses of brushes, plus the Blur and Smudge tools, allow you to blend colours and textures as on a traditional canvas. Here, the skin tones are softened using Blur, and the fine lashes are added using a fine brush.

Caricature: Charlie Chaplin

Final image

This caricature combines a very simple pen-and-ink drawing with a variety of found textures and sourced imagery. The bowler hat is a significant symbol of Chaplin as is the moustache, shaped in Photoshop from a scanned 'fur' sample. This project enables you to access a number of useful Photoshop tools for creating Charlie Chaplin, then manipulating the image with filters to present him within an early filmic atmosphere.

1 Begin with a referenced sketch of Chaplin drawn with a fineliner. Don't use any solid areas of black, instead leave every shape open for later texturing. The hat can be sourced from the Internet, or scanned from a book of fashion engravings and combined with the scanned line art on a separate layer.

2 When finished, the image is scanned into Photoshop, and a series of textures are added on a new layer behind the line art. These textures are found scans of existing materials, manipulated using a variety of filters in Photoshop, such as Noise, Blur and Free Distort. Add a block of suit mesh material behind the body, and some scanned fur – perhaps from a winter coat – for the hair and moustache.

3 Using the Eraser tool, carefully remove any of the scanned elements that are overlapping the line art. Alternatively, create a clipping path with the Pen tool, or use the Magic Wand tool on the line art layer to select the background white, before flipping back to the colour layer and pressing delete. This should remove any colour or texture outside of Chaplin himself. Next, colour in his skin and visible shirt in a pale blue. Place a feathered blue ellipse at his feet.

4 On another layer, shade the skin tones, shadows and textures using 15–30% black. Use a Custom brush set to dissolve on the shading of Chaplin's face, and an Airbrush effect with solid black for his eyebrows. Use the Hue/Saturation controls (Image > Adjustments > Hue/Saturation) to bring the textures into line with the blue of the skin. Keeping all of the colours within a tight blue palette captures the black-and-white movie aesthetic of Chaplin's films, as well as summoning up the hard-luck emotions embodied by the Tramp.

Caricature: Marlon Brando

Final image
This image is created using a combination of Painter, Illustrator and Photoshop. The painterly treatment added to a sourced photo of Hollywood actor-legend Brando provides a strong focus for the project. Centring on the power an image derives from contrast of texture and colours, a stylized shape-constructed body enables the Brando portrait to be connected and brought into an architecturally suggestive mesh of white lines and shapes. Simple, but very effective.

1 The head is created in Painter using an Acrylic Paints palette and Brush tools, working from photographic reference of Brando, which is abstracted and exaggerated so that the famous Godfather looks like a melting peanut. The head is then saved and imported into Illustrator.

2 The flat artwork for Brando's dinner-suited body is created on a new layer in Illustrator, using a variety of pen-drawn shapes and simple, flat colours. Keep this portion of the drawing iconic, so that the viewer's attention is drawn straight to the face. Even the triangle of the cummerbund at Brando's waist points back up towards his head.

4 Bring everything together in Photoshop for the final tweaks. Add a strong white line down the right-hand side of the head and figure to link the two disparate portions and separate the figure from the background. On a separate layer, create Brando's shadow by duplicating the Illustrator body, filling the selection with a gradient, and using Free Distort and Rotate to offset it to the right. Add the metaphorical pool of blood leaking from the city by filling a new shape with a gradient of black to red. Colour correct all the layers as necessary in Photoshop to fuse them into a complementary single image.

3 Create a new layer in Illustrator for the background. A few simple shapes, assisted by a Shallow Gradient, are enough to suggest the shadowy stage on which Brando's most famous character worked. Thin, criss-crossing lines and white gradients in rectangles are enough to suggest the windows. Note how the background pulls the image together by reflecting complementary colours from the body (the grey of the suit) and the head (the pink shadow).

Futuristic style

Vector cartoons are characterized by their sharp, even lines and smooth transitions of flat, solid colour. A modern theme, especially science fiction or fantasy, is well-suited to a vector package. In addition to clean, clear styling there is the chance to experiment with a wide range of colours and patterns which will give the right contemporary look to your cartoon. Since vector art can be infinitely scaled without losing resolution, your illustrations of 50m-tall (165ft) robots will look just as good at 5cm (2in) as on life-size posters! A hand-drawn sketch is the starting point for this project which is then constructed and completed in Adobe Illustrator.

Final image

This final image displays the many versatilities of Adobe Illustrator with a wide range of computer drawing techniques being coupled to a harmonious, pastel colour palette. Note how the various complexities of colour and outline contribute to a sense of depth in the image – the thicker lines and additional shading on the window-cleaning figure throw him to the absolute forefront, while the outline-less, two-tone colours of the buildings in the background push them back into the distance. The vapour trails of the rockets and skycars are simply line paths, expanded and blurred. When you are finished, why not experiment with different colour schemes using Photoshop's Hue/Saturation (Image > Adjust > Hue/Saturation) slider?

Tip: For complex coloured digital images, it is useful to make a rough colour sketch by hand first. Having this reference to hand will solve compositional and colour problems easily. To save time, print out small scans of your line art four-to-a-page and experiment with thumbnails before committing yourself.

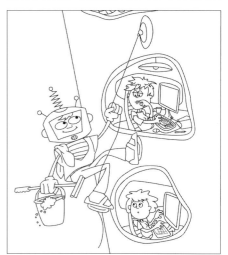

1 Make a neat pencil sketch of your chosen scene. There's no need to ink it traditionally at this stage, as you will be going over all of the lines digitally. Scan the drawing and import it into Illustrator.

2 Create a new layer (Layers palette > New Layer), and use the Pen tool to accurately trace around your pencilled image, following the original. Select the Pen tool and make sure that it is set to 0.1pt. This is not a job to hurry and will take a while to complete.

3 Select the outline with the Arrow tool and click on a mid-blue hue in the colour palette. Give the line character and shape by varying the line thickness – expand lines using the Direction Selection tool (white arrow) and go to Object > Expand. Create a new layer beneath the line layer, tint the background in blue and fill the character shape in pink.

4 Add the texture to the main building. On a new layer, draw three or four hexagonal shapes, tint them a paler pink colour and drop them on to the building as a fill, using the Pattern brush. This will cover the area in a repeating pattern of the shapes. Using more abstract shapes, without outlines, block in new buildings in the background, copying and pasting smaller shapes in to form windows. Rotate or 'free transform' a few of these so that they retain their individuality.

5 Finally, give the image greater tonal depth overall by adding detailed, darker areas of shading to the main figure and background elements. Create these shapes on a final layer and colour with the Opacity set to 30% so that the patterns show through. On the same layer, add white highlights to the windows using thick, stroke-like shapes. Select and delete the windows behind the office workers to reveal the sky layer behind.

Mass-producing characters

The original toy shape – Illustrator ◀
Draw freehand, and tint and shade in flat colours on a new layer that sits beneath the line art.

Copying and pasting the toy ▼
Adjust the scale each time so they appear to recede into the distance (Object > Transform > Scale). There are endless connotations – create a clone army of toys or an assembly line of automated machines delivering uniform toys.

The toy machine ◀
This is also drawn freehand, and coloured in gradated tones, to suggest industrial metal, rather than shiny plastic. The components falling into the funnels at the top of the machine are created by 'disassembling' your toy image – parts of the toys are selected, copied and pasted into place. Use Rotate or Free Transform to suggest motion and distance.

Touchy-feely textures

Digital technology allows cartoonists the freedom to play with surface decoration across a range of media. The projects on the next four pages centre on combining drawn animal cartoon characters with digitally created textures, photographic imagery or scanned fabric. The resulting 'real' fur or skin texture gives each cartoon a surprise edge. The surrealism is increased when this texture is manipulated in Photoshop. Where traditional collages rely on the disjunction between line work and texture for their effect, Photoshop allows you to literally paint with your found media, blending and integrating disparate elements like never before.

Woolly textures

1 Sketch a quirky representation of a sheep, enlarging the endearing facial features, friendly smile and curling lashes. At this stage, reference a suitable digital picture of a sheep (which focuses in sharp detail on the woollen textures), either scanned or downloaded from the Internet. Scan the line drawing at 200dpi or above and import it into Photoshop. Next, copy the line work to a duplicate layer and delete the original background layer. You are now ready to continue.

2 On the digital image, use the Clone tool (tool box) to select an area of the face texture on your chosen photograph (you can have this photograph open in a separate window to your line work). Hold down the Alt key and click the mouse on the photograph to select the Clone tool's starting point, and then paint freely on to your line work. The Clone tool works by linking two points, duplicating whatever is underneath the first. You can enlarge the area being duplicated by increasing the size of the Clone 'brush', as if you were painting – you can also adjust the Opacity and Hardness in the same way. Once you have reproduced this texture on the head and legs on the drawing layer, return to the digital image and select a point on the wool to start cloning.

3 When you have filled the wool with the appropriate texture, go to Filter > Distort > Ocean Ripple and add a ripple pattern to enhance the twisted texture of the wool. Finally, import a cloned selection of grass from the digital image and place it in a feathered oval section beneath the sheep.

Tip: Displaying real textures within a cartoon context offers your drawings real impact. Experiment with Photoshop filters to increase the wackiness of your images. Where you may think that a filter serves a limited purpose, it is often a surprise to find it has other unexpected uses too.

Final image
The success of the image depends on scanning a clear source reference at a high resolution. Photoshop allows you to test out all kinds of enhancements. For example, you can increase the contrast using Image > Adjustments > Levels, alter colours or adjust textures using the filters.

Scaly skin

 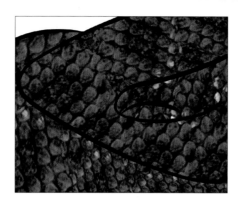 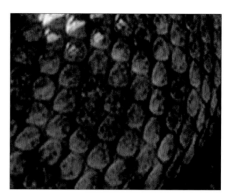

1 Draw the outline of the snake in Illustrator, expanding the line to thicken it and give a sense of movement. For the skin pattern scan a good-quality image of a rattlesnake and import it into Photoshop. Place the outline as a 'Multiply' layer in Photoshop and select elements of the snakeskin to clip out of the image using the Pen tool. Make a new layer and paste these behind the snake outline, then tidy up the edges.

2 Copy and paste your rattlesnake image as a pattern on the new layer until all of the areas of the snake are covered. Note how the pattern alters slightly as it curls around the body. At this stage, the repeat pattern will probably blend with little definition between the segments in places, but don't worry, as this will be refined and defined at the next stage. Choose a beady, glowing yellow for the snake's eye.

3 Increase the definition between the different segments of the snake on a new layer located above the line drawing. Adjust the contrast by using the slide bars on the Shadows and Highlights panel (Image > Adjustments > Shadows/Highlights). Consider the direction of the light falling along the length of the body. Here, a strong light source is almost directly above the snake serving to neatly delineate the underside of each coil.

4 Further refine the definition by making more detailed Marquee tool selections. Manipulate these using the Shadows/Highlights function under Adjustments and the Levels function under the Image menu (Image > Adjustments > Levels), where you can alter the dark tones, the light tones and the mid-tones.

Rough skin

5 Finally, separately colour the patterned bands in strong, yet lifelike hues such as blue, deep pink and bronze. Change these using the Hue/Saturation facility (Image > Adjustments > Hue/Saturation), by moving the colour slide bars in the panel.

Final image
The ability to be able to import textures with ease and open within a selected path area using Marquee and Selection tools is the key to this Illustrator and Photoshop combined image. Colours are easily changed or modified by adjusting the slide bars in the Hue/Saturation panel.

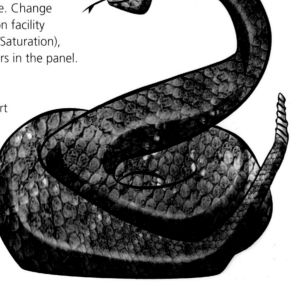

An elephant line drawing is scanned into Photoshop, darkened and then added as a new layer beneath. Basic shapes are drawn and filled with flat colour to render form through tone and highlights. An elephant-skin digital image is selected and used with a Brush tool to colour a new layer at 30% Opacity. This is placed on top of the coloured shapes. With the layers set to 'Multiply' the Eraser tool is used to clean around the outline. The flat colour-filled ellipse and rectangle background shapes are created on a layer placed beneath the rest.

Slimy skin

1 Draw the frog outline in Illustrator using the Pen tool and expanding the line (Object > Expand). Colour the line a dark green (Stroke > Colour) to reduce the harshness of the black line. Leave a white circle in the pupil for the highlight.

2 Create a new layer below the first and tint the outline in a light green (select colour from Swatches > use Paint Bucket tool to fill), with yellow and black for the eye. Make a shading layer, adding 15% black to the green.

3 With the basic drawing and colouring complete, Select All of your drawing and drag it from Illustrator into a new Photoshop window using the Selection (black arrow) tool. Create a new layer and add the coarse skin texture in selected areas, using different brushes to vary the texture.

Final image
Three layers are all you need to create a colourfully textured frog. From an initial Illustrator outline the image progresses into the addition of bold colours and skin textures, which can either be sourced, or developed with an array of brushes and filters. A shaded final layer placed beneath the frog assists the three-dimensional illusion and prevents the appearance of a hopping creature apparently suspended, floating in space.

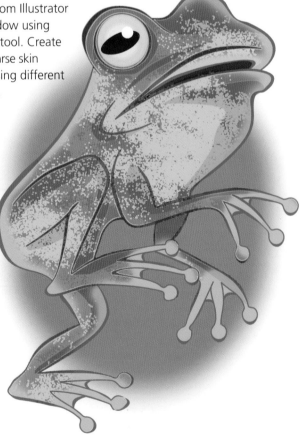

Experimental styling

Illustrator contains a considerable range of patterning and blending options. When you are satisfied with the final colour, you can begin to play with the patterns in the graphic style library. Don't worry if an effect isn't working – a click in a box will change everything.

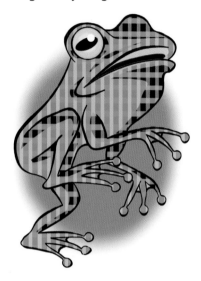

Check patterning ▲
This check pattern is selected from graphic styles, and the transparency palette set to 'Hard Light'. The pattern floats above the base colour and shadows without losing definition.

Distorted spots ▲
In this pattern, the spots are distorted so they appear to run across the curved surface of the frog's skin. Draw a circle, duplicate it as many times as you need, then distort it (Filter > Distort > Pinch) to achieve the desired effect.

Leathery wings

1 Scan your line drawing of a bat and open it in Photoshop. Scan a suitable piece of leather – a section of leather jacket is used here – and import it as a digital image. Using layers, place the texture layer beneath the line layer and remove the excess around the outline using the Eraser tool. Create a new layer for the background, beneath both the line and leather layers.

2 For the sky, select blue from the colour palette and add a tint that fades from dark to light using the Gradient tool. Draw a crescent-shaped moon using the Pen tool and fill it with a pale cream colour, which is softened with a feather of 10 pixels. Stroke it with solid white. Create and fill the blue-green hill shapes. Draw the grass texture using a custom brush in a lighter green–blue. Lines in a soft brush under either wing suggest movement.

Final image

This variation on the texture theme uses leather to simulate the bat's natural skin. The smooth surface of the leather will reflect the light shining through the scanner bed, giving its creases a 3-D appearance. The darkness of leather leads the choice of hues with deep saturation. Against these, the creamy white of the diffuse moonlight and grass blades offer the drawing a stunning lift.

Chicken feathers

1 Scan the key structural elements of this cartoon into Photoshop – a real chicken tail feather and body feather. During scanning, take time to adjust the Levels so that the image is strongly visible (Image > Adjustment > Levels). Doing so will capture the subtlety of the quills that are central to the project. Cut both feathers out with the Marquee tool and place them on separate layers.

2 On a new layer, arrange the scanned feathers to form the body shape, tail plumage and wing shapes. Do this by duplicating the feathers and also by using the Clone tool to clone smaller areas. You can overlap the feathers and make other adjustments using a number of new layers. However, aim to keep the image as simple as possible so that the basic concept of a cartoon chicken made from real feathers is not lost in a complicated design.

3 Add the beak, eye and comb on a layer above the last feather layer. These can either be drawn or created from a scanned digital image. Add a textured effect to the comb using filters. Go to Filter > Sketch > Bas Relief, then apply Filter > Noise > Add noise. On another layer add the drop shadow using a soft brush and adjusted feather (Select > Feather). Finally, add the scanned digital image of the wellington boots.

Final image

Real chicken feathers have been used to plume and preen the virtual chicken's identity. The clipping of such finely featured objects provides fantastic practice opportunities for refining your skills at drawing paths and cloning in Photoshop. Subtle use of filters is essential with such a delicate subject and soft brushes are necessary for dropping shadows and enhancing colours and textures.

Graphic novel style

Characterization for graphic novels is an in-depth and lengthy process. Once conceived as an idea, your character needs to be worked out on paper, and if you are choosing to create them digitally, transposed into graphic shapes and colours through Photoshop and Illustrator. Variations of style are wide and it is important to be aware of the techniques available in these programs. Background imagery is also important, but tantamount to success is your level of comfort with your creations. The average graphic novel is around 96 pages long, so be aware you could be working with the same characters for a long time!

Final image

For this urban narrative, Illustrator was chosen, for the simple duplication of bricks and also the creation of rigid, architectural lines, to help give the impression of an urban environment. A story needs to develop in a setting and this project considers the juxtaposition of the created scene and the narrative presented through the main figures.

Urban narrative: characters and background

1 Scan your outline pencils into Illustrator and create a Line layer. Digitally ink the outline using the Pen tool, contrasting the weights of line to create depth of field as shown here. Elements such as the windows and bricks can be easily duplicated by copying and pasting a single finished shape.

2 Drag the outline from the Illustrator window into a new Photoshop document. Drop some gradated colour fills into a new layer using the Gradient tool. Place this beneath the line layer. Having started with basic tones, you can now consider the best colour and texture choices for the image as you go along.

3 Now apply flat hues to the two characters using layers. It is best to use easily identified clothing and hairstyles in this first frame that can be duplicated and repeated throughout the whole storyline. Create the shadowing on a new layer to add depth and tone to the composition. Next, create the leaf by filling a new shape with a scanned leaf texture. The final touch is to add the dotted white path by manipulating and importing an Illustrator line.

Duplicating faces

Multiple characters are a necessary part of the graphic narrative and you will save time by creating a template library of key character styles for reuse in other frames. Keep the focus on body shapes, clothing and colours so that only a minor change of facial expression or body position is sufficient to place them with ease into the unfolding story. Take advantage of the compatibility of paint programs and work between them.

Photoshop style ◄
The line art was drawn directly into Photoshop with the Pen tool. The colours and textures were built up sketchily in layers.

Painter head ▲
The first heavily brushed head is drawn 'live' in Painter. Once the structure and rendering of the face are complete, it can be altered to create the second and third characters. They are created by altering

features, colours, shadows, mid-tones and highlights on new layers. Saving the structural layer as a template enables new characters to be produced quickly and efficiently, which can only aid your creativity and experimentation.

Illustrator style ◄
The line art from Photoshop was opened as a new layer in Illustrator, where it was drawn round, tweaked and coloured.

Illustrator: adjusted colours ◄
Adjusting the colour palettes as shown here is an effective trick for altering the mood of your piece.

Dramatic realism

1 Scan your simple outline sketch into Illustrator and go over it with the Pen tool to create a precise outline. A line that is too sketchy does not fit the graphic novel style and is harder to segment into selected colour fill areas.

2 In Photoshop, select and fill the drawn sections with flat colours from the palettes. Alternatively, apply gradated fills using the Gradient tool. Assume a light source on one side to add drama.

3 Enhance the realism by adding scanned photographs of real buildings and skies as background. Alter these images by Solarizing (Filter > Stylize > Solarize) to break them into strong slabs of colour, and experiment with the dissolve and overlay blends (layers palette) for added effect.

Final image
For this final image, buildings, a distant sunset and shadows have been added for dramatic effect and to put the character into the foreground of a slightly unsettling urban landscape.

Traditional fantasy style

The traditional approach to the comic supports hugely popular horror and fantasy styles. These require the ability to render the human form accurately in several active and emotive positions. For this style, it is still best to draw in pencil and ink – with a dip pen or brush – with the confidence displayed by the top artists of Marvel and DC Comics, but it is also fine to adjust and improve your line work in the digital arena. The key to effective horror styling is in the use of strong contrasts between areas of highlight and shadow, as well as the ability to create well-defined human characters that anchor the more esoteric or outlandish elements of your story or composition.

Final image

Here we have a 'Lizard Man' character, developed from an initial pencil sketch that is then inked in the traditional way, and imported into Photoshop to be defined in colour. Working digitally allows us to import a separate line drawing of a wind-blasted cliff to combine with our figure into a finished illustration.

1 The first stage of the illustration is a pencil sketch, in which pose and proportions are both defined.

2 Next, the Lizard Man character is inked by hand over the pencils, using a dip pen or brush and black Indian ink. The majority of comic books, though digitally coloured, are still drawn using the traditional pencil-and-ink method. The inking stage is when you define your light sources and strong contrasts, as well as apply organic textures with brush or nib. See how the upper left arm and curled right fingers are thrown back by being inked completely black. When you are happy with your inks, erase the pencils (be sure the inks are dry) and import the scan into Photoshop.

3 Create a fresh layer and fill it with the appropriate skin tones and clothing colours. To save time, you can select areas of the drawing using the Magic Wand tool on the line art layer, then flip to the colour layer and use the Fill Bucket tool or delete key to fill them with an appropriate colour. Create a twilight feel with a gradient tint fading from brown to yellow. Draw the moon on a separate layer by filling a circle with white. Back at the drawing board, create an image of a gnarled tree and cliff, and scan it into Photoshop on a layer behind your character to complete the scene.

Considering character profile

Profile is key to an effective narrative, and for this to work, your areas of shadow and light should flow from one to another, not overwhelm single areas of the page.

Dynamic characterization

Heroes and anti-heroes are often polarized in war and need to display dynamic traits, such as a ready-for-action stance, strongly defined body lines and totemic accessories.

Adding mascots ◄
Including the lizard considerably extends the dynamic stance of the Lizard Man. He not only extends upwards inside the vertical compositional plane but, helped by his leashed mascot, across the horizontal plane too. The giant lizard is a faithful copy from photographic reference. The head is turned back deferentially towards its master but the eye is drawn to make direct contact with the viewer.

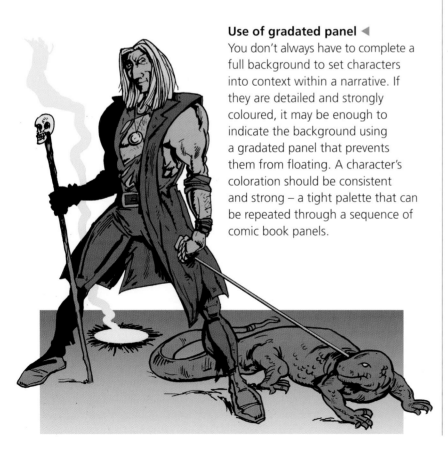

Use of gradated panel ◄
You don't always have to complete a full background to set characters into context within a narrative. If they are detailed and strongly coloured, it may be enough to indicate the background using a gradated panel that prevents them from floating. A character's coloration should be consistent and strong – a tight palette that can be repeated through a sequence of comic book panels.

Power stance ▲
Drawing a character with a commanding stance instantly conveys his ability to wield power within the graphic narrative. The turn of the body is essential: the side tailing away into shadow emphasizes the leading side.

Tattoos and body paint ▲
Photoshop is excellent for branding warriors with tattoos and body paint. This blue 'woad' face mark is added by using a Pen tool to draw the shape on a new layer, then selecting it and creating and adjusting Colour and Opacity using the Hue/Saturation sliders.

Manga style

Although 'manga', and its animated cousin 'animé', contain as many different art styles as you will find in western comics, there are certain characteristics that have become synonymous with the form – chief among them the vibrant 'big eyes, small mouth' school. Rooted equally in the Japanese illustrators of the 19th century and the imported cartoons of Walt Disney, 'manga', which is Japanese for 'comic' or 'whimsical pictures', is home to a far broader range of subject matter than we are used to in our graphic novels, from universal themes of love and lust, power and politics, and the journey into adulthood, transposed to any number of exotic and everyday locations, to series rooted in the worlds of sport, mahjong, videogames, music, business and politics.

Tip: Manga is an art form predicated on extremes of motion, punctuated by occasional, poetic stillness. Even 'at rest', your characters will need to be dynamic, poised for the next exaggerated spring into action. Everything is made to feel that it is bursting forth from the page.

1 Start with a pencil sketch that uses the main features associated with manga females: high cheeks, large, round endearing eyes, sensuous lips, square jaw and 'choppy' hairstyle. Include the basic outlines of your setting.

2 Scan the drawing and import it into Illustrator. Use the Pen tool to digitally ink over your pencil outline, expanding the lines as you go where you feel it needs most emphasis, such as in the definition of the hair shape, and in the curves of the body and limbs. In this example, we will be colouring using a 'cell-shaded' style familiar from the majority of animation, so don't add any areas of solid black for shadows as these tend to overpower the subtleties of colour, which keenly denote this unique style.

3 Drag the layer into Photoshop and select the areas to fill with flat, bold colours. Draw random shapes on the clothing for the camouflage patterns using the Pen tool, and fill with the appropriate flat colour. Add shadows to the skin by adding 15% black on another layer. Add white highlights to the grey weapons and on the body.

4 On a different layer, create the background scene, accessing all the major techniques for Photoshop painting, a gradated blend for the sky, a drawing line and fill for the setting sun, and blended paint strokes for the white vapour trails heading for space.

Final image
Here's a fusion of the western and manga cartoon styles. A tough, well-armed female soldier confronts a bizarre alien life form on a distant world. The soft gradient of the background pushes the bold character forward, while a motion blur effect on the alien creature gives the impression it has just vaulted up out of the topsoil.

Manga figures

While exaggeration is crucial, manga figures are still based around a confident understanding of human anatomy. Body shapes are fit and stylized – but in a more down-to-earth way than classical superheroes – with large heads, narrow waists, small, nimble feet and streamlined, fashionable clothing. Your figures should all be clear individuals, with unique hair, build, costume and accessories – check that you can tell them apart, even in silhouette.

Manga action ▼
Extreme poses and angles are the order of the day when capturing an action moment. Examine sample manga artwork to see how even moments of emotional drama are imbued with hyper-kinetic energy. Manga makes heavy use of motion lines to sell the concepts of speed and movement. These can be time-consuming to replicate in Photoshop or Illustrator with the Line tool – but will prove much less hassle than using a fineliner and ruler.

Creating the male face ▲
The line work is created in Illustrator, with a stylistic expanded line, and the areas of shadow and definition are kept to a minimum so that he appears contemporary and flat-featured. This simplicity is distinctive of manga.

Creating the female face ▲
The line work is created in Illustrator, using a rough pencil sketch as the base. A stylistic, expanded line lends weight and interest to the hair, eyes and brows. Note that the elements of the face still conform to the 'eyes halfway down' rule, even though they are out of proportion with one another. Basic tones are applied in Photoshop.

Defining the female face ▲
The unreal blue of the eyes draws our attention to them, and forms the focal point of the face. Shading is achieved with a strong two-tone shadow. Highlights are kept to a minimum – on the lips and on the reflections in the eyes. Pay extra attention to the shading and highlights of the hair, as it is easy to make this look like a plastic wig if you are not careful.

Defining the male face ▲
The next stage is to soften the drawing considerably in Photoshop using the Airbrush tool, especially for blending the subtle highlights on the skin and hair. The final result blends cartoonish two-tone colours with naturalistic shading to suggest a more mature art form.

Science fiction style

The digital revolution has brought a new sophistication to the genre of science fiction, demanding no less skill than traditional methods, but substantially reducing practice time. Photoshop filters and the ability to be able to blend semi-translucent layers have considerably influenced the techniques and the resulting outcome. Digital trickery and futurism (the prediction of a future world and its attributes) go hand in hand. The cartoonist has the freedom to conjure up imaginary scenarios that are painlessly realized via keystrokes and mouse commands. In the digital art future in which we live, creativity truly knows no bounds making possible the imaginary worlds of our furthermost dreams.

Mixing media

1 Scan the rough coloured sketch of the time traveller and import it into Photoshop. Draw over the lines with the Pen tool, expanding as necessary as you go. Convert the black outline to a soft blue line via Image > Adjustments > Hue/Saturation. Drag the image into Photoshop and render it in simple colours on a new layer below the line art, using a range of brushes from the brush palette.

2 With the idea set, spend some time dropping in careful brush blends within the variably stroked outlines. Pay attention to smaller details, such as the shadows beneath the control console and the underside of the sleeves. Adjust the Hue/Saturation to add reflected light to the face and use the History brush to soften colours in the final stage.

3 Draw the clock faces on the floating instrument panel as a new Illustrator document, using the Ellipse tool for the dials and the Pen tool for the hands. Stroke the outline in white. Create a single dial, and then duplicate, scale and free distort it to form the rest. Import a scanned or digital galaxy image into Photoshop and create the vortex through the Twirl filter (Filter > Distort > Twirl). Drag the dial into the Photoshop window and sit as a new layer on top of the galaxy background. Duplicate and distort the dials by pulling out the shape from the points on each clock face.

Final image

This image effortlessly blends the past and present into an amalgam suitable for a man torn out of time. The simple, cartoonish line drawing and industrial-era machinery contrast sharply with the swirling, all-digital maelstrom of the timestream in flux, literalizing the 'collision' between two different media.

4 Set the long line of dates on a spiral line in Illustrator using the Pen tool and the Text tool. Drag this into the Photoshop document to sit above the dials layer.

Android

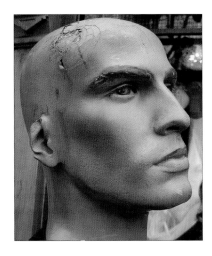

1 Select and scan a suitable photographic image for the head. The blank eyes, smooth modelling of this mannequin's head, and the surface cracks make it a perfect choice for a humanoid robot.

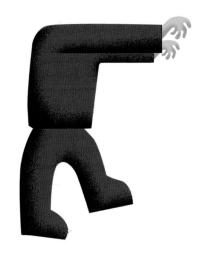

2 In Photoshop, draw the simple body shape using the Pen tool. On a new layer, select and fill the drawn shapes in grey. For the darker grey shadows set the layer blend to 'Dissolve' and select a deeper hue. This blend results in a smoother tonal sweep, but with plenty of contrast remaining. Add a soft textured effect to the clothing by experimenting with filters – try Filter > Noise > Add noise. This will differentiate the clothing from the smooth, strongly featured head. Use the Colour Dropper tool to select a shade from the digital image of the head to colour the hands.

Final image

Photographed objects can form the major part of a Photoshop cartoon. The dead, soulless gaze of the mannequin is perfect for the aloof robot, and easily allows the rest of the body to be drawn and attached. The joining of the two images is made simple through layers, the depths of hue and texture through limited use of colour slider bars and filters.

3 Combine the two image layers so that the head rests on the body. Use the Hue/Saturation sliders to adjust the head layer to a greenish-grey hue. Make a gradient background tint on another layer which fades upwards from deep green to black. Create the lightning on another layer using a white brush line, feathered and stroked with green set at 5 pixels. Make the 'airwave' cloud by selecting a patch of green, painting it with a brush, then modifying it via Filter > Halftone > Circles. Finally, draw the shadow under the feet using the Ellipse tool, softened with a feathered edge. Place the shadow on the layer beneath the figure.

Sci-fi options in Painter, Photoshop and Illustrator

Knowing how to juxtapose images and programs can give you a great result in a short time-frame. Opting for small vignetted illustrations is an effective way to make the whole task simpler.

Crazy scientist ▲
The head is created and distorted in Painter before positioning on to a hand-drawn pen sketch scanned into Photoshop. Experimenting with filters works a two-part magic process. First, use the Pointillism filter to create the test tube fumes, then alter them further with the Curl and Twist filters.

Space travel ▲
This light-hearted image expounds the notion of interstellar travel using the gravitational pull of black holes. It is drawn and tinted in Illustrator, and would be perfect for a popular science magazine.

Mixed media collage

Combining real-life and drawn elements is a technique much practised by cartoonists and other illustrators. You see it used in all kinds of media, from spot newspaper illustrations to graphic novels, strips and fine art. Animation has used this merging of real and imaginary worlds to great defamiliarizing effect for many years, with the early Disney films *Mary Poppins* and *Bedknobs and Broomsticks* among the first to fuse whimsical cartoon worlds with traditionally shot actors.

In those pre-digital days, it was a highly complex achievement involving numerous artists and endless hand-drawn images placed on top of extant film footage. Today, whether for moving or static images, vector and bitmap computer programs make it easy to seamlessly mesh the 'real' and 'unreal' together.

Final image

This magpie is so persistent and successful in its efforts to get its wings on the shiniest of baubles that it has reached out of the cartoon world and into our own. The metaphorical, cheeky quality of the drawing makes this illustration of avarice much easier to swallow, while the use of real jewellery is a simple and effective addition to the picture that reinforces its value.

Tip: Pocket cartoons, graphic novels and comic strips are all suitable media for collaging 'real' photographic images with drawings.

1 Lightly sketch your design and scan your drawing at 300dpi. Import the scan into Photoshop. Choose Image/Image Size and then reduce the file size by resizing the resolution to 100dpi. Make sure that the 'Resample' box is ticked. Drag your resampled image into a new Illustrator document set to the same dimensions. Double click on the layer and reduce the Opacity to 50%, then rename this layer 'Trace' and lock it. As it is just a sketch, feel free to add placeholders for the elements that will later be collaged digitally. Here, we've started with a bird selling watches. The pleasure of working digitally is that it allows you to change your mind – and the direction of your piece – late into the process.

2 Create a new layer above the trace layer and name this 'Line'. Using the Pen tool (set to black, no fill, 1pt), trace over the sketch until the drawing is complete.

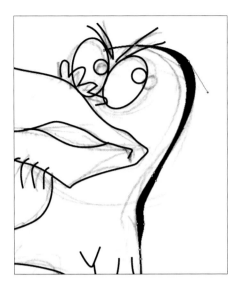

3 Expand the line to make it more interesting by choosing Select All > Object > Expand. Use the Direct Selection tool to drag anchor points of the line apart. Use the Pencil Smoothing tool to reduce excess points.

4 When you are satisfied with your line drawing, import it back into a new Photoshop document, set to 300dpi. Set the layer to Multiply, name it 'Line' and lock it. Make a new layer behind the line art.

5 On the new background layer, begin colouring basic shapes using the Paintbrush tool set to 100%. Erase stray colour using the Eraser tool. Gradually build up the blocks of colour.

6 Use the Lasso tool to isolate areas for special treatment, such as the tail. Airbrush the feathers using a 200-pixel soft brush to blend the colours.

7 On a new layer, create the shadow by filling an ellipse selection, with feathering set to 20 pixels. Use the Eraser tool to remove overlapping grey on the feet.

8 Scan and import the jewellery. Use the Transform tool to scale each object. Erase the scan backgrounds using the Magic Wand and Eraser tools.

9 Place each object on a separate layer and when you have placed enough, make another new layer above the background layer. Use this layer to add the shadows to the beak, feet and behind the jewellery, which will give the image depth and tone. Darken the colours in the shadow areas by about 15%. Select each one using the Eye Dropper tool, go to the colour slider palette and move the slider a little to the right. Draw the shadows with a soft brush.

Tip: Use layers to help you to build depths of colour and mark within your compositions, or to juxtapose graphic elements. The best way to think of layers is as sheets of transparent acetate which lay one on top of another allowing you to see what lies above and below. Layers can be easily created or duplicated and lifted into the most suited position.

Using advanced colour theory

The digital production of images offers a limitless number of colours to play with, and a similarly wide range of methods with which to apply them. However, sometimes a simpler, restrained approach will net you the best results. Images decked out in subtle tones can often be the most effective. By not dazzling or crowding the eye, they allow the viewer to concentrate fully on the narrative. The considered use of small areas of hue – known as 'spot colour' – brings focus to bear on the most significant elements. All digital painting programs lend themselves to creating images in a limited span of tints and tonal 'keys' – the name given to tones which all fall within a small range of colour increments. Over the next four pages, we shall explore the benefits of spot colour and limited palettes, as well as more advanced techniques including ambient glows and expressive textures. Why not try colouring the same image multiple times, summoning different moods through different palettes and techniques?

Using hue with a two-colour limited palette cartoon

1 Draw the ink and charcoal sketch. Scan the image into Photoshop and duplicate the background layer. Drop a neutral colour layer, set to Multiply, on top of the image, to act as a background hue. Create a new layer named 'Spot Colour Overlay', set it to Multiply, and use the Marquee tool to select areas to colour: the sign, car keys, lips and dress. Fill these with a red-based brown, adjusting the colour using the Image > Adjustment > Hue/Saturation sliders on the red channel.

Final image
The strength of a two-colour limited palette cartoon is evident here, and the highly selective use of the hue works harmoniously with the quality of the line and charcoal tone with no conflict of elements. The careful blending with soft brushes working closely in relationship with the buff-tinted paper, lifts the texture of the image and evokes the gritty atmosphere.

Limited pastel palette

1 Import the same scanned drawing into a new Photoshop document. Scan some buff textured paper and save this to a new layer, set to Multiply, placed on top of the drawing layer. As before, select the shaded charcoal areas to colour with the Marquee tool, this time focusing on the background of the drawing. Convert these areas – the car, the cactus, the burger joint – to sepia, using the Hue/Saturation sliders.

2 Photoshop's expressive colour ranges allow you to easily match the moods and effects you are trying to create in your images. Here, using restraint and minimalism, select a range of pastel tints from its colour palettes. On another new layer, colour the remaining main elements and their details, bringing the two characters forward from the monotone background. For the sky and clouds, employ a soft brush, blending the edges of each block of colour so that they appear to merge into the tint of the buff paper.

Final image
Using a limited pastel palette for this more muted final image has been key, allowing for a slightly changed, possibly more positive overall tone of the cartoon, but it is also important to retain the black outline around the figures to help pull them out from the sepia background. You must also keep your colour shading minimal, allowing the original charcoal lines to do your toning work for you.

Colour swatches

The Adobe packages contain a wide array of swatches to help with choosing colours. The opportunity to see the colour families grouped as they are on the artist's colour wheel makes light work of selecting complementary tints and shades.

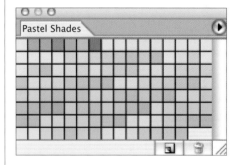

Pastel shades ▲
These shades are typical of the types of colours that result when white is incrementally added to a pure base colour. By clicking on a tile in the palette, you can select a hue for use with the Brush or Pen tool.

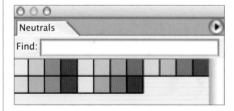

Neutrals ▲
Colour neutrals are variations of grey which have a hint of brown, green, blue or red as their base. They work in harmony with most other colours.

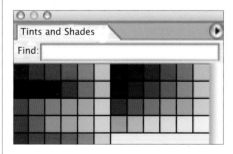

Tints and shades ▲
If you were mixing up tints and shades in paint, the tints would be colours with a hint of white added and the shades with a hint of black. Shades are the colours most commonly used for shadows and tints for highlights.

Gritty shadows and glows

1 Sketch an exaggerated cave scene, contrasting the manic form of the caveman with the relaxed cavewoman. Note the bold, outsized hands and feet on the caveman, which draw attention to his flailing and stomping. Scan the sketch into Illustrator, and outline using the Pen tool. Create a tight selection of colour swatches in brown, blue and flesh tints down one side – use these for later colour selection in Photoshop.

2 Import the drawing into Photoshop as a new layer. Below the line layer, paint a new background layer in dark blue. Colour the characters, smoke and cave elements with flat colours, shadows and highlights as before. To create the glow effect on the flame and cave entrance, 'knock back' the black line around each element by selecting the line on the line art layer and colouring it a slightly darker shade of the flame using the Fill tool.

3 On another layer positioned on top of the flat colours, add the shadows and blurs. For the gritty texture of the dark cave shadows, select a 300-pixel soft brush from the Brush palette and set it to Mode > Dissolve. Spray this brush around the arc of the cave mouth and curved walls. The same brush, coloured white, can be used to add flavour to the border of the background.

Final image
Here, a combination of a variety of elements contrasts the frenzy of the caveman with the relaxed demeanour of the cavewoman. The motion blur on the arms, the glow of the fire and the harsh light outside are simple effects which all serve to inject depth and dynamism into the image.

Ambient glow

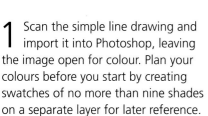

1 Scan the simple line drawing and import it into Photoshop, leaving the image open for colour. Plan your colours before you start by creating swatches of no more than nine shades on a separate layer for later reference.

> **Tip:** Colour swatches play an important part in understanding the continuation of sequences in cartooning. Always choose base hues that work well together to create the correct mood, and be sure to include them in all the frames making up the running frames of the story.

2 Create the dispersing background glow emanating from the lamp by selecting the Gradient tool and setting it to 'Radial Gradient'. Choose the two colours to gradate from the swatches – white to mid-brown. Click to choose the central point of your radial blend, and draw the line to indicate the extent of the first colour (in this case, white). The longer the line you draw with the Radial tool, the greater the percentage of white in the final mix, and the larger the 'bloom' in the centre of the gradient. The shorter the line, the larger the percentage of brown.

3 Use the Lasso tool to isolate areas of the face, arms, T-shirt, lantern and body. Fill these with a mixture of linear and radial blends as appropriate, on new layers, using the Gradient tool. In this example, we've used radial blends on the face and left arm, to reflect the gleam of the lamp, while the other elements have been coloured with a linear gradient. On another layer, paint in the trees, grass and barn using flat colours and a soft brush for the occasional highlight. Place each new layer you create above the overall background radial gradient layer.

4 When you are satisfied with the gradient and colour layers, Flatten (Layer > Flatten Image) and duplicate them. Set the duplicated layer to 'Multiply' – this will intensify the depth of your chosen colours and throw up the contrast between the areas of light and dark more keenly. Make the bright lights of the fireflies with a soft, round brush (size 30) dabbed on to the image in a combination of white and creamy yellow hues. Draw the flight trails using the pressure-sensitive stylus pen on the drawing tablet. This will give you maximum control over their movement and direction and enable you to taper the line as it trails into the distance.

Final image

The completed cartoon shows the kind of depth of field and atmosphere that can be accomplished with a very limited palette and a judicious use of gradients. Note how the use of complementary shades and gradients draws the eye across the image in an unfamiliar direction – we focus first on the strongest light source, the lamp, then on the glow on the boy's cheek, then follow his upturned eyes to the true centre of the image – the fireflies themselves.

Monstrous textures

Inventing an imaginary creature allows you to give free rein to your creativity. Monsters are excellent subjects – the only rules that apply to them are that they must be both freakish and scary to some degree – but remember too that the most successful monsters of print and screen are sympathetic to some degree. They present the ideal opportunity to merge aspects of fantasy and reality, creating a range of digital Frankenstein's monsters for you to bend to your will. The advantage of using the computer as your main tool is that it allows you to experiment freely while still being able to roll your image back to any part of the process. Essential elements, such as shape and scale, colour contrasts and textures, can be tried out to your heart's content, without fear of compromising the final result. Don't be afraid to throw on new filters or play with as-yet untouched settings – the perfect piece may arise from a happy accident.

Creating a sympathetic 'monster'

1 Build the broad face in Painter, using layers of paint in your favoured medium, working from mid-tones to shadows and highlights. Pay attention to the furrowed, horizontal lines at eyebrow level and around the thin-lipped mouth. A strong centre-line down the brow and nose, formed of shadow, grants the image weight and depth. The face is lit from either side by diffuse light sources, so pay attention to the different coloured highlights (blue on the left, orange on the right) that suggest each light. Strongly angle the cheek muscles up to meet the nose, and note the thickset shadows beneath the brow and mouth.

2 Import the head into Photoshop. On a series of new layers, create a body using real, scanned garments – or portions of fabric cropped and shaped in Photoshop using the Lasso tool. Smooth any misfitting edges between cloth and head with the Blending tool.

3 The shoes are created from shaped portions of a scanned texture. Place scans of real hands, scale them in size and make them more purple by adjusting Hue /Saturation. Tangles of string, scanned, form shoelaces, and images of rusty bolts complete the Frankenstein cliché.

4 To give this misunderstood monster a hiding place, scan a photograph of a dilapidated barn and place it on a new layer behind your creation. To give the barn an eerie, unreal quality, add a new Adjustment Layer > Hue/Saturation and bring the Saturation down to -60. Scale the barn so that it sits behind your monster, with the creature breaking out of the rigidity of the boxed background to add interest to your composition. Like Frankenstein's original 'mixed-media' creation, this monster is just crying out for animation! Why not experiment with different facial expressions or a range of hands?

Final image

This creature is a combination of painted features, found textures and scanned photographic elements. Switching between Painter and Photoshop allows you to intermingle a variety of source materials in an organic fashion. Using the slider bars of the Hue/Saturation adjustment layer, you may wish to completely change the ambience of a benign scene to something far more sinister – or you can also brighten up the image by intensifying all the colours.

Gnarled skin

1 Scan a pen and ink drawing of a morose monster into Photoshop. Apply a flat purple hue to the creature on a new layer beneath the line layer. An easy way of doing this is to select the white area outside your creature on the line layer, choose Select > Inverse, then switch to your colour layer and Fill the selection. If your image is a joined-up ink rendering such as this, you'll find this method quicker than painting the whole image with the Brush tool.

2 Apply the lighter and darker purple tones using a soft brush on a layer placed above the flat colour. Apply a linear gradient blend of red/green above this layer, set to 'Hard Light' (in the layer blending box and scroll down to 'Hard Light'). This creates a glow effect in the area of the two-colour blend. Finally, use the Eraser tool to remove excess colour around the monster – or select the white areas on the line art layer, flip back to the gradient layer and press delete.

3 Add a skin texture using the Craquelure filter (Filter > Texture > Craquelure > Distort > Spherized). Use a soft blue-white/mauve-white brush to add the fine detailing on the eyes and horn. Draw the bristly hairs using a small, hard brush. Finally, on a new layer beneath the figure, spray on an ellipse with a soft feathered edge as the monster's shadow.

Final image

Only a handful of 'real' features in a drawing are required to convince the viewer of its veracity as a character, no matter how outlandish the physiology. Here, the well-rendered reflections of light on the creature's eyes, and the bristling hairs and textured skin, are enough to bring life to a horned, ambulatory bowling ball.

Quick digital monsters

Photoshop is perfect for developing monstrous characters, allowing you to experiment with a wide range of styles, and summon a cast of spooky characters for use in cartoons, comics, graphic novels or simple animations. Simplicity of design is the key – build your creations from exaggerated and distorted geometric shapes. Start with an identifiable silhouette, and work back from that.

Monster faces ▲
These Photoshop portraits are rapidly sketched using a stylus and drawing tablet. Lay down a face shape first and fill it with flat colour. Employ the Brush tool with a darker hue to tint the shadow and facial details. Add interest by using a textured brush.

T. Rex ▲
The expanded line of this Illustrator drawing is stroked in hues of blue and green. It is imported into Photoshop for texture and colour: Filter > Pixelate > Pointillize (cell size 5) is applied to a gradated blue-green tone. Filter > Render > Lighting Effects > Texture Channel (set to green) is the next step, set at 60% 'Mountainous'.

Metallic surfaces

Like monsters, robots offer your imagination the opportunity to run wild. As long as they display mechanical workings, robots can consist of shapes, colours and textures in any configuration you prefer. Robots in popular fiction can range from benign automata to laser-wielding machines of death, so it should be easy to find a droid that fits the mood of your project – contrast the robots of Asimov, *The Wizard of Oz*, *Terminator 2* and *Doctor Who*, to name but four. The only thing that cartoon robots have in common is their metallic 'skin', which can be achieved through a wide variety of effects, to replicate the different methods that went into their various processes of construction.

Creating a metallic 'skin'

1 Scan a simple pencil sketch of a weeping robot, and import it into Illustrator. Trace over the lines with the Pen tool, and use the Direct Selection tool (white arrow) to expand the line by pulling on selected points (Object > Expand).

2 Import the Illustrator outline into Photoshop. Create a new layer for colour and set it to 'Multiply'. Paint the drawn areas in flat colours of blue and grey. Fill the buttons on the chest unit with bright primary hues. To add depth, create a new shading layer and place it above the colour layer. Pinpoint your areas of shadow and stroke on the darker shades using a soft brush. Don't worry about the metallic texture or the contents of the puddle at this point.

3 Select the white background portions of the image on the line art layer, using the Magic Wand, and use Select > Inverse to capture the robot. Create a new layer, selecting 'Use Previous Layer To Create Clipping Mask', and fill the mask with a blend of reddish-brown and black. Apply the Pointillize filter (Filter > Pixelate > Pointillize) with a low cell size – this will add the simulated texture of rust. Make sure all your colour layers are set to 'Multiply' so that the rust blends with your colour textures. Erase parts of the texture so that some of the original blue-grey shows through. Flatten your image so far. Create a new layer from a Clipping Mask of the puddle, duplicate your coloured robot and use Transform (Edit > Transform > Flip Horizontal) to create the mirror image. Now distort it using the Liquify filter (Filter > Liquefy). Add highlights on a new layer to selected areas of the surface.

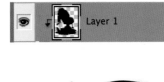

Final image

This image employs multiple layers beginning with the simple outline drawn in Illustrator. Photoshop layers help to build depths of colour and these are vital to shade in certain areas to create the 3-D illusion on a 2-D digital drawing. The metallic textures, which bring a touch of realism to the robot, are applied effectively by actually erasing colour and texture from a 'Clipping Mask', the layer covering the whole of the image.

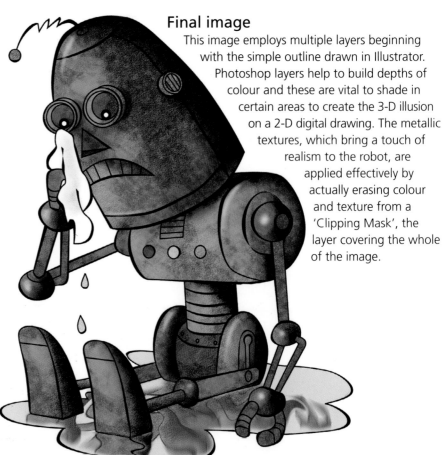

Metallic shine

1 The outline of the robot siphoning a drink of oil from a vending machine is drawn directly into Illustrator. This method forces an economy of line from the beginning. The work involved encourages you to keep detail to the essential minimum, which makes for 'cleaner' and more readable art.

2 Import the line drawing into Photoshop, and place a flat colour layer below the line art. Choose four or five flat metallic colours to fill the outline – in this example, a selection of greys, mingled with blues and browns. Select and fill the shapes using the Magic Wand and Fill tools.

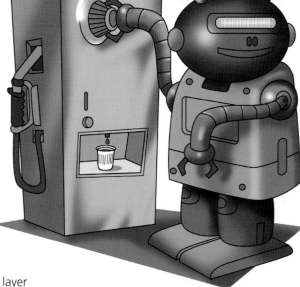

3 Create a new layer above the flat colour layer to add form to the drawing. Use a soft brush or airbrush to add shades, and alter the Opacity of the different tints to produce the subtlety required. Make another layer above the tone layer for highlights. Don't be afraid to build up to the brightest highlights in steps. Create the whirling antennae by filling two circles in red. Select each individually with the Magic Wand, making sure your background colour is set to white, and apply Filter > Sketch > Halftone Pattern > Circle to them.

Final Image

The simplistic shapes and basic shading on this image nonetheless combine into a finished piece that has a great deal of character and dimensionality. The shadow of the claw arm draped across the robot's chest, along with the burnished tones of the vending machine, adds depth, while the blues and the reds help define and contrast the conscious robot with the unthinking drinks vendor. The easy effect of the flaring antennae adds a further dash of personality to the illustration.

Alternative automatons

Creating robot figures is a fun way of combining shapes and experimenting with colour and expression as well as movement. See just how easy it is to anthropomorphize even the most outlandish of shapes with the addition of a pair of eyes!

Simple robots ▲

Illustrator is the ideal choice for quick-fire designs or the execution of simple cyber characters. Shapes are quickly and easily drawn, selected, coloured and duplicated – and the Pathfinder tool groups them into a single shape.

Robot power ▲

This Illustrator/Photoshop image blends the cliché of the superhero with a robotic shape. The cape and trunks clothe the body in familiar, yet unnecessary attire (for a robot!), and the massive mechanical forearm embodies the concept of superior force.

3-D Illustrator effects

The ability to create hyper-real 3-D objects in Illustrator opens up a wealth of new opportunities for image creation, whether combining a 3-D shape with hand-drawn characters or generating intriguing, abstract landscapes. Though limited in comparison to a fully featured 3-D program, these effects can add an appropriately thrilling new dimension to your drawings, when used correctly. As with all new filters or tools, use it wisely and sparingly for the most impact. First though, a light pencil sketch can get the imagination firing.

Final image

This psychedelic fantasy landscape challenges the viewer's perceptions with its shifting depth of field, hyper-realistic background elements and humorous alien figure – who alone has evolved to navigate the surreal landscape. Not bad for a quick Illustrator sketch.

Abstract landscapes

1 This project is created directly on the screen, so plan it before you begin. Make a light pencil reference sketch of an otherworldly composition and decide which elements will be applied using the 3-D tool. Remember to keep all object shapes simple, and revise your thoughts until you are satisfied.

2 Go live in Illustrator now and create a 3-D shape using the Effect filter – go to Effect > 3-D > Extrude and Bevel > Complex 1 Bevel (and choose 50pt extrude depth). Repeat the process to make a variety of simple shapes, which you can then group together to form the alien tree.

3 Create a simple stick shape to form the tree trunk and turn it by applying the Revolve tool (Effect > 3-D > Revolve). Place the tree on a gradated colour background of yellow and purple formed using the Gradient tool.

4 Create the spheres from a drawn semicircle (always made to the right of the vertical guide) using the Revolve tool (Effect > 3-D > Revolve), and place them on a number of layers both in front of and behind the tree. Draw the alien outline on a separate layer, applying a yellow and green gradient fill. Apply the green circle pattern using the Halftone filter (Filter > Sketch > Halftone Pattern > Circle) on a new layer set to 'Multiply'.

Imitating plastic

As before, plan your composition and layout with a quick sketch before taking the plunge into Illustrator. We're going to create an iconic image of a 3-D flying saucer, rendered to look like a plastic toy, laying waste to a 2-D city. The 3-D Revolve tool is perfect for creating simple, symmetrical, plastic-looking items – so it's great for capturing the nuances of early sci-fi toys.

2 Use the Effect > 3-D > Effect > Revolve tool, with a blue shading colour selected (these options can be found by clicking the 'More Options' button in the Revolve options menu that appears). Add extra highlights to your shape as necessary, and make sure that the 'Cap' option is set to 'solid' (the left of the two Cap options, located next to Angle in the Options box). Click OK, and Illustrator will create a plastic-looking saucer in three dimensions.

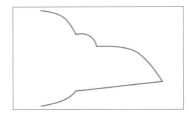

1 Draw the saucer profile in a new Illustrator document using the Pen tool. Remember to only draw half of it, to the right of the vertical guide. Stroke the outline using a 1pt pink colour fill.

3 Create the setting using the Simple Illustrator Pen tool to shape and colour buildings placed against a gradient background of red to reddish-brown. Place the saucer on a layer above the buildings and import the image into Photoshop. Using a 20-pixel brush yellow outer line and a 5-pixel brush white inner line, create the laser beam, holding down Shift to draw a perfectly straight line. Add the impact flash in the same way, starting with large yellow and white brushes for the explosion, then stroking out thin white points.

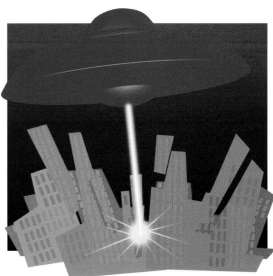

Final image

This picture playfully tweaks its nose at the science-fiction concept of aliens invading from another dimension, as the power of the third dimension is literalized: the chunky toy saucer vaporizing a 2-D cardboard city. Whether escaping from its box into the wider world of the toy store, or asserting the box-office dominance of CGI cartoons over their traditionally animated brethren, this flying saucer certainly means business!

Creating depth with drop shadows

This project provides another strong contrast between 2-D and 3-D, but this time it is the setting which is fully realized, and the figure that is drawn to resemble a cardboard cut-out.

1 Draw a very simple chair shape directly in Illustrator and fill it with flat colour. Now add Effect > 3-D > Revolve > Plastic Shading. The shiny plastic appearance instantly transforms the flat shape into rounded 3-D.

Final image

An image such as this, where an abstract, iconic cartoon is integrated with a rendered item, could be used to draw attention to a product or service – a new range of sofas, perhaps, or a deluxe departure lounge. The 'realism' of the item draws the focus of the image to it, while the simplicity of the figure allows for the maximum affinity with viewers – the simpler the cartoon, the more people will identify with it.

2 On a new layer, outline a seated figure using the Pen tool. Fill all the sections with flat colours and place this layer above the chair. Create a third, drop shadow layer and place it between the inflatable and the flat figure (Select the Figure layer, choose Effect > Stylize > Drop Shadow, with a low value for the X and Y offsets – the other options are up to you). This lifts the flat figure and adds to the illusion that she is seated.

Tip: When you have mastered the basic functions of the Revolve tool, experiment with diffuse shading and create more ambitious custom colour palettes.

Retro style

Every period in history is reflected in its art, and popular graphic styles speak volumes about the culture and music of an era. Fashion tends to look back at past styles, and new trends often borrow from earlier times to create 'retro' styles, either reproducing colours and patterns associated with specific periods or amalgamating retro influences into a new 'fusion' style.

The computer is a tool that's perfect for such imitations, as program filters and simple techniques can successfully reproduce the cruder appearance of nostalgic ephemera, such as jazz record sleeves, with their coarse halftone colour screens and mis-registration.

Final image

For the final touch, scan some yellow paper, torn at the edges, and place it above the entire image in 'Multiply' mode. Now this battered LP sleeve could easily be stumbled across in a thrift-store. Although worn around the edges, this image still has effortless cool. If you want more realism, use the Brush tool to add highlights to the sunglasses, choosing the uppermost layer. Now all you have to do is choose a band name!

Using retro influences

1 Do a light pencil sketch in the 1960s' graphic style, simplified and stylized, with legs and arms tapering away to small wedge feet and hands. Scan the drawing. Changing the line colour to blue in Photoshop may help you keep track of which lines you have overdrawn in the next stage.

2 Overdraw the sketch in Illustrator with the Pen tool set to 1pt. Expand and drag the lines to add variable weight to them (Object > Expand). The lively character of the lines suits the freeform, musical nature of the cartoon, while the open areas are perfect for large swatches of colour.

3 Import the drawing into Photoshop and select a limited palette of colours appropriate to the period. The muted blue and orange deliberately lack the vivid brightness of contemporary hues. The saxophone is a toned-down grey. Apply these hues as flat colours, then proceed to the next stage.

1950s' advertising imagery

1 Pencil a quick sketch and scan it into Illustrator. Outline the figures using the Pen tool, expanding the lines (Object > Expand) as needed. Stroke the lines with sober, dark versions of the colours you will fill them with: orange for the skin tone, deep blue for the dress and so on before importing into Photoshop to fill the areas of flat colour. You may find it easier to import the black line art into Photoshop, fill the areas of colour and then colour the lines with the Fill tool on the line art layer, using the Lasso tool to isolate sections of the image. Apply tonal brushwork on a layer placed above the flat colour.

2 Outline and colour three rectangles of wallpaper in Illustrator. The wallpapers are formed from bold and simple shapes which can be copied, pasted and rescaled or rotated quickly from a detailed image. Curve the bottom edge of each rectangle, and import the wallpaper image into Photoshop, placing it under your completed figures. Create a soft grey shadow oval with 20% Opacity and position it beneath the feet of the figures.

Final image
The strong blues, turquoises and browns and cheery 'big-headed' cartooning style create a period image that's perfect for illustrating an article on home décor – whether in the 1950s or the present day!

4 On a new layer, apply separate gradients to areas of the hair, scarf, shirt and trousers. Apply Filter > Sketch > Halftone Pattern to the gradients to convert the gradient pattern into dots. On a further layer, airbrush in black shadows and add Noise (Filter > Noise > Add Noise) for texture.

5 To get the retro effect of pinstripe wallpaper, create a square on a new background layer and fill it with orange. Now draw a single blue stripe on a layer above and duplicate it across the width of the orange square. For a brighter, more modern image, simply change the wallpaper colours.

Spot colour head

The distinctive mis-registration of colour layers is a key feature of 1950s' and 1960s' graphics, the result of a limitation in the offset lithographic printing presses of the time. Replicating this imperfection grants retro-style images authenticity.

Out of register ▲
The head is drawn directly in Illustrator and the line expanded at various points. The flat colour is applied deliberately to misalign with the outline edges.

Applied halftone filter ▲
Still in Illustrator, the drawing is extended to include the body, limbs and giant toothbrush, all set against a plain yellow circle with an outline stroked in red. In Photoshop, a Colour Halftone filter is applied on a new layer (Filter > Pixelate > Colour Halftone), then partially erased to leave a dotted effect around the edges.

Integrated characters

Cartoons can be elaborate and still remain focused. A beautifully researched and executed setting elevates a simple frame to the level of high art. In the history of animated films many of the artists responsible for their richly detailed backgrounds were successful painters in their own right. In the pre-digital days, painstaking hours were spent fleshing out dense foliage – a task that can now be achieved in a fraction of the time using computer shortcuts.

When attempting a jungle scene, nowadays you do not need to paint every vein of every leaf to offer the impression of density. Working in layers on Photoshop or Illustrator allows you to simulate depth, building up areas of detail that recede into a distant haze of soft silhouettes. Learning to pare down detail as the layers recede and work from strong colours at the fore to washed out colours at the back is the key to success.

Final image
Every element of the background works in unison to direct attention towards the main character. Framed by the simple greens of the foliage, the jungle man is shunted to the fore of the image by the resultant negative space. The lineless silhouettes of trees suggest depth without overlapping with the figure, while the yellow background gradient behind his torso is another subtle cue that draws the eye's attention.

Using background setting

1 Sketch the jungle man in pencil, resting on a tree trunk and gripping a vine, with a curious snake dropping into the scene. Block in areas of the jungle, but don't go into great detail at this point – leaving the intricate line work for the inking stage adds more spontaneity and life to the final drawing.

2 Ink over the drawing in dip pen and black Indian ink, filling in all the details of the frame of dense undergrowth. Add shading to the main elements – the figure, snake and tree trunk – with sparser tonal marking elsewhere. Leave the canopy and upper background as a simple keyline. Leave the black-and-white picture to dry, erase your pencil marks and scan the finished drawing into Photoshop.

4 On a new layer, strongly tint the snake, man, log and clothing. Keep the colours simple and light, and add only the minimum of shading. Colour the foliage in the fore- and middle ground with a flat, overall green. Add sketchy shadows and highlights with the Brush tool, complementing the detail of your inked drawing with thin lines of soft colour. Finally, on a further background layer above the gradient, brush in the tree silhouettes, using a soft, medium-sized brush. Tint these in a lighter green so they fade into the background.

3 On a layer beneath the line art, apply an intense, gradated radial light seeping through the canopy: make this simply as a circular gradient, bleeding from yellow to green with the Gradient tool.

Fully painted depth of field

1 Draw a cute and comical monkey using a dip pen and black Indian ink. Apply extra pressure to the pen nib around the simian's head and body, increasing the line's width and character.

2 The range of brush tools in the Painter application is ideal for the impressionistic background. Use acrylic brushes to lay down soft, opaque strokes that can be smudged using the Blending tool. Keep softening the marks until all the hard edges have disappeared. Add some fine detail to suggest grass stalks in a thinner brush.

3 Import the background image into Photoshop and apply a Gaussian Blur (Filter > Blur > Gaussian Blur) to the foliage to suggest distance. Import the monkey and branch into a layer above the background and tint both in flat colours on a separate layer, adding a second shading tone to the fur. Allow the dark green at the feet to show through.

> **Tip:** As a rule of thumb, the more dense the illustration, the simpler the colouring needs to be. It is the definition of the line work that will 'carry' more of the image.

Final image
Surrounded by solid black lines, the monkey pops out of the image, as if photographed with a shallow depth of field. In contrast to the flat, sharp colours of the monkey the soft foliage recedes, adding a range of hues and shapes without over-whelming the subject of the cartoon.

Cartoon symbols

In the graphics world symbols are often used as a means of communication. Easy-to-read images can present all kinds of messages: they are often connected to specific products or appear as brand logos, or are used to give directions or instructions in public places or on a website.

Creating a pared-down, instantly readable, recognizable symbol is a skilled undertaking and thinking economically is no small task. The target for the cartoonist is to reduce an image to its essence and produce a result with as little visual fuss as possible. Producing symbols using a computer graphic package is ideal because of the naturally clean look of a digitally generated image.

Creating a graphic logo

1 Make pencil sketches of your ideas for the mechanic character. Maintain an unfussy line which will be suitable for redrawing in Illustrator. Scan the sketch and open it in Illustrator. Trace around the outline using the Pen tool and expanding some line widths.

2 Import the image into Photoshop and select a simple mono-chromatic palette – white, pale blue and darker blue. A monotone logo still has a tightly designed power. On a new layer beneath the line art layer, fill the different shapes in your image with flat colour. Create small spots for the cheeks using a pale blue fill in two circular selections.

3 Make the cartoon look more like a logo by dropping in a circular background. Draw this using the Ellipse tool, holding the Shift key down to constrain the proportions so that the height and width of your selection remain the same. Place this layer behind your line and colour layers, so that the figure is projected to the forefront. Apply an 8pt white stroke around the character. As seen in the final image, shadows can make a lot of difference to the perceived depth of your symbol. Here, Layer effects (Layer > Layer style > Bevel and emboss) have been applied to the background circle.

Final image

This logo for a company of mechanics is the perfect fusion of clarity and personality. The limited colour palette focuses the attention on the form rather than the rendering and the comically enlarged spanner and overalls leave the customer in no doubt of the services offered, while the pared-down cartoon face adds friendly reassurance. The logo would be equally at home above a garage, on headed notepaper or as an embroidered badge.

Anthropomorphized objects

1 Sketch your final idea, firming up pencil lines to check their graphic strength. Scan and import the drawing into Illustrator. Trace over the sketch using the Pen tool. Experiment with line widths and sizes using the Expand tool (Object > Expand).

Final image

This symbol is perfect for an anti-littering or recycling bin awareness campaign, or for boroughs creating literature on littering for schools.

2 In our first colour interpretation, the lines vary between thick and thin to add character. The colours are filled with flat yellow and green, with highlights running vertically down the front edge of the bin and on the cheek dimples for added interest. To help the bin show up more against the white background, and to tie it together as a logo, a yellow ellipse with Opacity reduced to 30% is placed behind the bin on a new layer.

3 This alternative version of the same image reduces the detail and complexity in order to make it read more cleanly. A uniform 3pt line runs around the whole of the figure, the background elements have been entirely stripped out and the two colours are completely flat, with no highlights. This makes it perfect for rendering on a bin as cut-out areas of colour formed from a soft plastic such as EVA. Evaluate the success of your various versions.

Simple logo

1 Draw the cup and saucer shapes in Illustrator with the Pen tool. Create the aroma swirl using the Spiral tool. Add a grey tint to fill.

Final image

A clear logo is essential to promoting a product with success. This simple coffee cup sends a message that is universal in its appeal.

2 Re-colour the grey silhouette cup and aroma spiral in black and transfer the image into Photoshop. Draw a picture box with rounded corners on a new background layer. Select and apply a medium-blue colour fill from the colour palette. Create a final layer with the Gradient tool set to circular. Apply a warm orange colour and place this at the front.

3 Experiment with filters, effects, line strokes and fill colours to explore different results. The original drawing does not change throughout this process but the results can profoundly alter the look of the symbol. Here, the cup is enhanced with coloured horizontal bands. A Glow layer (Layer > Layer style > Inner glow/Outer glow) is enhanced by the black background.

Design variations

To guarantee the most effective results, consider several options, even if you're happy with your first attempt.

Reversing out ▲
Try reversing out the images by converting the black line to white. Does this render the image more effective?

Glow effect ▲
This striking glow effect is applied in Photoshop using Layer > Layer style > Inner glow/Outer glow.

Enhancing the stroke ▲
Illustrator can be used to enhance specific details of an image, such as this spiral of coffee steam as a 4pt yellow stroke.

Texture, depth and perspective

Slithering, scuttling or crawling creatures enjoy much more favourable press in the land of cartoons than they do in real life. The horror and revulsion with which they are usually met tends to evaporate when they are personified as wide-eyed, good-humoured and lovable – no matter how many their legs or how sticky their thorax.

The irresistibility of bugs as cartoon characters is compounded by the fact that they make fascinating and rewarding subjects for the artist. Coming as they do in a plenitude of sizes, shapes, textures and colours, they give plenty of opportunity to explore and exploit the range of tools and effects in Illustrator and Photoshop to the full. Perhaps the best thing is that, given the immense number of species and variations, you should never run out of inspiration for new bug-eyed, bug-ugly characters.

Final image

A handful of out-of-the-box textures and filter effects combine to create a varied and engaging snail with only a small amount of effort. The colourful bubble-wrap texture on the body creates a slimy and exotic feel, while the swirl of colours on the shell at once complements and stands apart from the line work, like a pop-art painting mounted on the creature's back.

Applying colour and texture

1 Create an Illustrator line drawing of a snail with strong, rounded shapes to give plenty of character. Expand the Illustrator shapes (Object > Expand) at points along the line to bring it to life. Add humanistic features, such as expressive eyes to the tips of the feeler stalk, or a mouth with a knowing grin.

2 Import the drawing into Photoshop, create a duplicate layer and clear the original. Draw a simple square on a new layer and fill it with a flat, yellow-ochre colour. Add broad, brushy strokes of various colours on top, using a special-effects brush from the Brush palette. Don't be conservative about your colour choices – keep them complementary, but don't feel constrained by realism.

3 For the shell pattern, apply the Twirl filter to the shell colour layer (Filter > Distort > Twirl) and size the spiral. Remove excess pattern by selecting the relevant areas with the Magic Wand tool on the line art layer, then changing back to the colour layer and pressing delete. Apply a 'bubble-wrap' pattern from the Styles palette to the snail's body, then select the front of its belly and apply streaks of black and yellow, before blurring them with Filter > Blur > Motion Blur. To create the reflection, flatten, duplicate and flip the image, then apply Filter > Distort > Ripple and some Motion Blur.

Rendering and perspective

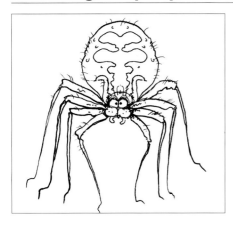

1 Consider the shapes and overall structure of the spider and draw it using a dip pen and black Indian ink. Scan and import into Photoshop.

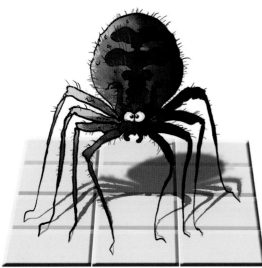

Final image

Bristling with tiny hairs and stalking across the bathroom floor towards the bath, there's no question this cartoony spider would get an arachnophobe's back up, even if he is waving hello with his palpi. The bulging, crossed eyes, however, soften the blow and make this alien insect relatable!

2 Select the whole outline apart from the eyes using the Magic Wand or Lasso tool and apply a gradient blend of light- to mid-brown across the width or length by drawing the gradient line in the appropriate direction. Pan in closer using the Zoom tool and tidy up any stray colour around the outer line using the Eraser tool or Magic-Wand-and-delete method.

3 To give the torso a realistic sense of depth, tint the markings in various shades of brown, yellow-ochre and a range of dark reds. On a new layer select the filled areas to Fill, then apply Filter > Render > Lighting effects to adjust the intensity, texture and shine of the arachnid markings.

4 Construct the tiled floor on a new layer. Create a single grey square and go to Layer > Layer style > Bevel and emboss. Now right click on the layer and choose Convert to Smart Object. Duplicate the layer to make the tile into a square of 12 tiles, and merge the tile layers into a single object. Now put the object into Perspective (Edit > Transform > Perspective). Finally, create the spider shadow by duplicating the creature on to a new layer, darkening the colours to black using Image > Adjustments > Levels. Distort the shadow using the Shift key and Transform, then apply the blur filter. Reduce the shadow's Opacity to 70%.

Textured soil

As with all cartoon creations, environment is the key to 'selling' your characters and making them believable. Here, we'll integrate an earthworm with a realistic patch of soil.

1 Create a coloured outline drawing in Illustrator, expanding the line in certain areas. Import it into Photoshop and apply soft airbrush modelling to the body segments. Tint each segment on one layer, then create another layer above it and add the white highlights.

2 To form the textured earth square, paint a few blobs of brown on to a rectangle and apply the Craquelure filter (Filter > Texture > Craquelure). Put the rectangle of earth into Perspective using the Edit > Transform > Perspective command. Apply the earthworm shadow to the soil using a soft brush on a new layer in Multiply mode underneath the worm's colour layer. Add the movement strokes using a suitably soft brush on the white highlight layer.

Final image

The detailed rendering on the worm's body, and its well-integrated nature with the background, results in a compelling 3-D image. The manner in which the perspective is framed also makes the worm look as if it has burrowed into the page.

Composite images

Digital methods offer artists the opportunity to create images which can look good enough to eat. Whether created for use in product development, advertising, food magazine articles or as commodities within a graphic novel, these realistic foodstuffs trick the eye and tempt the stomach. The high degree of realism is achieved through the use of layers, filters and 3-D tools, combining separately rendered 'ingredients' in a deliciously digital mimicry of real-world cooking.

Creating a realistic image with filters

1 For the first part of this image, draw a circle in Photoshop and fill it with a three-part gradient of yellow, white and light brown (Gradient tool). Select a soft brush, and use it to add a few touches of a darker brown around the edge to simulate a burnt crust. Apply the Craquelure filter (Filter > Texture > Craquelure) to the whole to express the cooked dough.

2 Create the base of tomato sauce on a new layer as a circle of rich red with deliberately rough edges. Select a darker red hue, and add a thickly scribbled edge to the whole disc using a solid brush. Apply the Plastic Wrap filter (Filter > Artistic > Plastic Wrap) to the central part of the circle so that the tomato appears to glisten. This may look unfinished but will be covered up by the next layer.

3 Add the yellow cheese layer above the tomato layer as a slightly smaller circle of pale yellow. Keep the edges loose and fussy, extending the odd tendril out over the tomato layer. Apply dabs of mid-yellow across the cheese surface and use the Liquefy filter to swirl it like melted cheese. Add a slight 3-D effect to elevate the topping, using Layer > Layer Style > Bevel and Emboss.

4 Create a salami slice, then duplicate it and arrange 18 images on the surface. For a more natural look, overlap cheese on to the slices using the Clone tool. Apply small brush dabs of brown and green over the surface to represent a sprinkle of herbs and seasoning. Work these tiny, short strokes randomly over the whole of the pizza. Now flatten the image and correct the perspective using the Transform tool.

5 Use the Selection tool (Lasso or Polygonal) to cut a wedge shape out of the pizza and move it to a new layer above the rest. Use a light yellow brush to add strings of cheese, adding shadows in mid-yellow, and using the Smudge tool to smear and blend. Place the whole pizza on a black background to make it stand out and add a few wisps of steam using a soft, white brush. To take the image further, why not recreate various toppings, illustrate a pizza knife lifting up the slice or composite the pizza image into the box art of an Italian food brand of your creation?

Final image

Utterly tempting, this image is a great example of how simple shapes and colours can produce professional results when coupled with a selection of filters. This pizza is made entirely of manipulated circles, layered atop one another, but judicious application of filters and brushes renders it almost photorealistic.

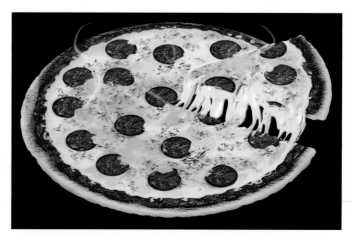

Combining 2-D and 3-D elements

1 Construct the cone in Illustrator and apply the 3-D filter (Effect > 3-D > Revolve) using the settings shown in the screengrab below. To map the image of stars onto the object, click the 'Map Art' button and apply the settings shown at the right. You can map any image you like on to a 3-D object, but it must be stored in the Symbols palette in the document you are working on – you can add a layer or group to the Symbols palette just by dragging it in: it will then be selectable from the drop-down menu in the 'Map Art' option.

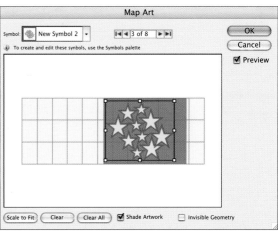

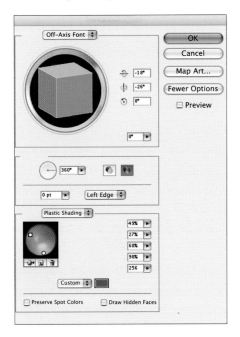

2 Import the cone into Photoshop. Draw a single French fry, duplicating and rotating it using Edit > Transform and the Rotate function. Spot the fries with tiny strokes of white to indicate salt and apply Filter > Render > Lighting effects to selected areas to add realism. Select areas of the cone with the Ellipse tool where fries are overlapping it, then go to Image > Adjustments > Invert and delete.

Final image
The specialist 3-D tools of the Illustrator program are perfect for artificial design elements such as this carton, while Photoshop excels at the organic elements of this illustration. Combining the two lends your images variety, novelty and – appropriately – flavour. Try duplicating the same process to different effect – why not start by rendering a tub of popcorn?

Layering ingredients

Preparing food often involves building up ingredients in layers. The snacks illustrated here demonstrate clear parallels with digital layers and filters that can be used to mimic texture. Why not take a cue from fast food and create your illustrations in a modular way?

Hamburger layers ▼
The three hamburger images show how easily Illustrator layers can be stacked, duplicated and rearranged. This method is an effective way to mass-produce simple images and reuse portions of a drawing without them looking stale. The examples would make great additions to a new menu or website.

Layered lolly ▲
The ice is sketched in Photoshop using the Pen tool and filled with a yellow/red gradient. The stick is made in the same way and placed above it. The stick part inside the lolly is selected, moved to a layer above and set to 'Multiply'. Filter > Distort > Ripple is applied to distort the view slightly, and a few gradient-blended, liquid drops are added.

Between fantasy and reality

This subject matter is as old as the fairy folk themselves. Goblins, trolls, leprechauns, pixies, imps and fairies good and evil all play the central role in tales and myths where morality needs to be explained. They inhabit the magical side of cartooning where, like the best superheroes, they can interact with any situation – real or imaginary. Employing Illustrator and Photoshop together provides the ideal vehicle for bringing together the fantastic and the realistic in a believable, yet make-believe fashion.

Merging cartoons with photos

1 Make a pencil sketch of your fairy's pose. You will also need a digital photograph for the backdrop, which may influence your figure's interaction with her environment. When you are happy with your composition, scan the sketch into Illustrator and draw over the outline using the Pen tool, stroking the line in blue and expanding the line on the sweeping curves.

2 Import the Illustrator outline into Photoshop and choose a range of blue hues using the picker from the Colour palettes. When making your selection, consider contrasting the weights of tones. For example, a mid-blue, flat tint for the hair is best teamed with a much paler hue for the face, but one that is within the same range, such as warm blues.

3 Tint the crown yellow, the lips red and the neck and skirt ruffs mauve. Now add the 'magic glow' all around the fairy's outline: select the whole outline using the black arrow Selection tool and add a feather of 10 pixels, with a soft 10 pixel brush, in a creamy yellow. This effect will be more visible against the background.

Final image

This fusion of the digital photograph and simple cartoon typifies the world of fairies – at once overlapping and apart from our own. The white glow around the fairy figure keeps the real world at bay and draws our attention to the fact that she doesn't belong – as if her winter-blue skin and wings weren't big enough clues! The outlandish purple sky and ripple effect in the water further blur the definitions of 'our' world and 'hers', while the trees mirrored in the water only add to the unsettling, otherworldly, but strangely soothing effect.

4 To create the background, select and duplicate your digital photo of a tree (Image > Duplicate). Flip the image (Image > Rotate Canvas > Flip Horizontal). Bring them together on a Photoshop document large enough to fit both versions side by side. Drag the flipped photo on to the first image, which will import it as a new layer. Line up the two images accordingly. Alter the overall colour to blue (Image > Adjustments > Hue/Saturation).

5 Create the ripples in the still lake using the Ripple filter (Filter > Distort > Ocean Ripple). Now position the fairy over the background, where she conveniently hides the join in the middle of the two photographs. Her glow, previously invisible on the white background, will finally come to life – add a reflection of it in the water. Lastly, tint the sky lilac using Image > Adjustments > Hue/Saturation.

Sharpening the focus

The fairy character and little devils here exemplify the irresistible temptation of chocolate cake.

Wicked fairy ▶
An ink drawing is scanned and taken into Photoshop and combined with an imported digital picture, which is cut out using the Selection tool and placed below the line layer. The figures are selected and tinted in flat colours and a separate layer is made for the 300-pixel soft airbrush background.

Humorous contrasts

1 Make a clear pencil outline sketch of the leprechaun (note the contrast of the bulky body and tiny feet). Scan and import the outline into Illustrator. Carefully trace over it with the Pen tool, expanding the line where appropriate to thicken it (Object > Expand). When you are satisfied with the drawing, import the image into Photoshop.

2 Note the limited colour range here. The green of the skin is close to brown, with the red outline, beard and wings deliberately selected to complement it. The red spots on the toadstools mirror the beard and tie the picture together.

3 Add tone overall by selecting areas for darker tinting using a soft brush. Then add Filter > Texture > Grain. Finally, tint an elliptical background shape.

Final image
This version of the popular, male, Irish equivalent of fairies known as a leprechaun is a simply hued mix of jollity, luck and goodwill. The heavyset figure with tiny wings brings to mind the myth about the aero-dynamics of bumblebees!

Legendary lighting

Ancient myths, such as the Greek legend of the Minotaur, offer perfect material for creating the cartoon or comic strip equivalent of a Hollywood blockbuster. As with all good movies, the mindset of a director is needed to facilitate the cartoon and find the high point of the narrative so that an audience is exposed to the full potential of the drama. With cartoons, this is achieved not only through the cropping and composition of images, but also through the use of a range of dynamic and dramatic lighting effects, such as fire, lasers and torches. Computer technology offers the digital cartoonist the chance to unleash high-impact effects on an audience by applying a selective range of simple tools and filters.

Colour and spot lighting

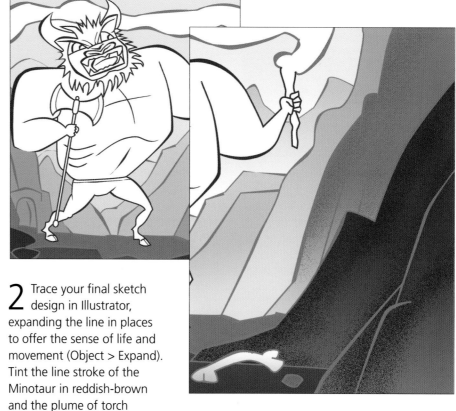

1 Give careful consideration to the way of presenting the character and situation to best achieve the effect you are aiming for. Looking at other cartoonists who specialize in your chosen area, and adopting some of their styling, may help. 'Thumbnailing' the illustration – experimenting with bold compositions in frames the size of postage stamps – may help kick-start the process by forcing you to think about shape and framing rather than fine detail. Sketch your final outline carefully in pencil. Scan the image into Photoshop, and apply a simple gradient overlay to give yourself an idea of where the central light source will fall.

2 Trace your final sketch design in Illustrator, expanding the line in places to offer the sense of life and movement (Object > Expand). Tint the line stroke of the Minotaur in reddish-brown and the plume of torch smoke in pale blue. Tint the larger rock masses in flat colours taken from the same tonal range.

3 The mood of the cartoon is dependent on the subtleties of tone used on the rock strata. Take the image into Photoshop and apply these darker gradations within selected areas on a new layer, using low-Opacity brushes set to Dissolve. Place this layer above the flat colours so that the colour still shows through.

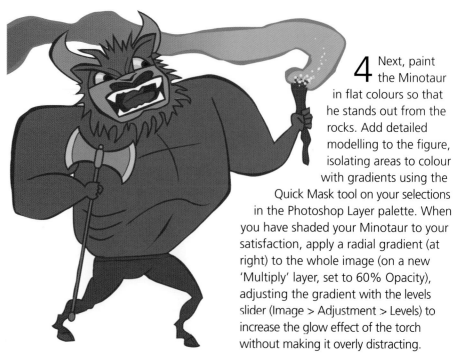

4 Next, paint the Minotaur in flat colours so that he stands out from the rocks. Add detailed modelling to the figure, isolating areas to colour with gradients using the Quick Mask tool on your selections in the Photoshop Layer palette. When you have shaded your Minotaur to your satisfaction, apply a radial gradient (at right) to the whole image (on a new 'Multiply' layer, set to 60% Opacity), adjusting the gradient with the levels slider (Image > Adjustment > Levels) to increase the glow effect of the torch without making it overly distracting.

5 Give the scene an eerie light with a gradated overlay of blue and brown in 'Hardlight' mode applied across the image. This will intensify and darken shadows at one end of the scale and highlights at the other. Check over the image and tweak colour imbalances. Finish the image by brushing in additional flames on the torch and the reflections in the Minotaur's eyes.

Final image
This image is a masterclass on creating mood and drama. Blues and browns tightly grip the picture, drawing the eye to the red flame, its fiery reflection in the Minotaur's arm. The creature is framed by the gulley, pushed to the foreground by the cool blues of the receding trench, while dark gradients push in from all sides.

Torchlight and laserlight

1 This pastiche of a 'Judge Dredd'-style character begins as a careful Illustrator line sketch, including the background setting, which is then imported into Photoshop. Using Quick Masks to isolate the figure, apply a blue-and-red gradient overlay to it, leaving the background untouched. Erase any excess colour from around the edges of the figure.

2 Colour the background scenery in the same assortment of gradients and flat colours, giving the cartoon an overall dark and gritty mood. The key feature of the picture is the laser gun blast, so use the Lasso tool to roughly select the area intended for it. Fill the area with a pink-and-white gradient.

3 Add a thin, sharp line up the centre of the gradient with a small, soft brush, holding down the Shift key to ensure it is straight. Use Filter > Render > Lens Flare to model the intense light. Repeat for the torch, with a blue gradient. Add red and blue highlights to the figure on a new layer. Add the stars with a 100-pixel brush set to Dissolve, with a Flow of 20%.

Final image
This image uses a time-honoured cinematic trick of using torchlight and/or laserlight to provide lighting and focus, in addition to giving a grittier, more ominous feel to the cartoon.

Aerial perspective

The illusion of using colour to represent pictorial depth is known as aerial perspective – which should not be confused with aerial viewpoint, or the bird's-eye view! For centuries, painters have explored the relationship that exists between colour and distance. In nature, the scattering effect of atmospheric particles results in distant objects appearing bluer and washed out. Art, however, gives you licence to use any colours you wish. As a general rule, stronger, more primary coloured shapes grab immediate attention and are perfect for foreground elements, while paler pastel hues recede into the background, furthering the illusion of depth.

Photoshop is a great program to use for the creation of a cartoon with a receding background. As well as the extensive choice of colour palettes, numerous filters can be used to soften shapes, reduce focus by blurring or alter textures to suit.

Final image

The colours may be emotive rather than realistic, but the eye has no trouble reading the distance in this image. The base and forefront of the picture are anchored with full-black shadows and heavy lines, while line weights diminish to nothingness towards the rear – the farthest objects lack keylines, becoming vague shapes in the autumnal sky. The complexity of the textured pattern on the man's coat brings him to the fore, as the eye slows down to decode the zigzags.

Using colour to create depth

1 Make a simple outline pencil sketch that contains all the basic information for the illustration. Try to keep the shapes simple and bold. Scan this image into Photoshop.

Tip: When inking over your pencils, don't try to replicate every nuance of the original sketch. Aim to capture the same freshness of line that was in your sketch – draw inspiration from that, rather than being a slave to your pencilled blueprint.

2 Duplicate this background layer and set it to 'Multiply' before deleting the original background. Create a layer for colour beneath the line art layer and roughly block in the various colours, using the Brush tool at 100% Opacity and Hardness. Reduce the Opacity of the pencil line layer to 50% using the slider. Now draw around the line in black, tracing it with a fine brushstroke, making sure your line is loosely and freely stroked for a more painterly effect.

3 With the line work complete apply a fill pattern (Edit > Fill > Use > Pattern) to the coat. Make a simple arrangement of diagonal lines to create the basic 'herringbone' pattern. Tidy any pattern overlaps that stray outside the coat outline with the Eraser tool. A Gaussian Blur filter (Filter > Blur > Gaussian Blur) on the buildings in the background distorts the pixel pattern to create a different, yet subtle texture. Sections of the background are erased with the History brush to ensure that the foreground remains in focus. As a final, tonal adjustment, you may wish to use a selection of gradients applied on layers above the whole image (as on the previous spread) to tie the colours together. Experiment with layer options – 'Multiply' and 'Hardlight', particularly – in order to give a subtle boost to the colours.

Changing the scene

The same subject can be moved through the seasons by changing colours or filters. Simply slide the Hue/Saturation controls: Objects > Adjustments > Hue/Saturation. Isolate the figure with a Lasso tool/Quick Mask selection, or reinstate his colours with a History brush.

Diminishing with distance

1 Create a single robot figure in Illustrator and tint it in Photoshop. Duplicate the figure and then scale each duplication using the Scaling tool.

Tip: Try this particular distance technique with other subjects. A mountainous landscape offers stunning pictorial depths, with trees and peaks receding into the background, becoming paler and more blurred as they diminish.

2 Reduce the scale of each robot, altering the colour too. Shift the hue range further towards the recessive blue/mauve palette. Also adjust the colour Saturation (Object > Adjustments > Hue/Saturation).

Final image
This robotic assembly line demonstrates the ease with which aerial perspective can be put into practice, and also underlines the effectiveness of the digital domain at mass-producing characters. With a copy of Photoshop and a representative character, you can produce an army of thousands in minutes. Just remember, for non-robotic characters, try and introduce quirks or imperfections to differentiate your cast of thousands.

3 Select the three robots behind the foreground figure, one by one. Apply Filter > Blur to the first and increase the level of blurring to the second and third. This technique is an effective way of increasing the illusion of receding depths.

Pet portraits

Digital painting and rendering software offer excellent tools for creating pet caricatures – with their wide range of naturalistic media options, you will find it easy to capture the intricate details of furs and hairs – whether building up textures in layers of digital paint or utilizing bold colours and repeating patterns for a more abstract effect. The digital domain also offers an endlessly reworkable way to build drawings from brief colour sketches into fully rendered pieces of art.

Pets make great subjects for the cartoonist, offering a host of endearing, quasi-human traits that can be exaggerated or massaged into an amusing or characterful illustration – just think how many successful syndicated cartoons feature household pets as their stars! Enlarged noses, muzzles or ears can expose an animal's inner character, while large, emotive eyes anchor the drawing and make it relatable for human readers. Body shape too is an important indicator of cartoon

personality – a rotund pet dog reads as contented and friendly, while a skinny, stalking cat comes across as aloof or even suspicious.

Experiment and draw inspiration from family pets or animal photos in magazines, attempting to capture the nuances of their personality in a cartoon form. Work from very quick pencil sketches, elongating, squashing and exaggerating key features, before embellishing and adding detail in Photoshop and Painter, as below.

Curious dog caricature

Final image
Several effects increase the effectiveness of this image of a dog on the prowl. The exaggerated muzzle and ears – both overlapping the edges of the frame – draw attention to the canine's senses of smell and hearing, while the cocked ear directs the eye to what has caught the dog's attention – the cat, rendered shadowy, abstract and symbolic atop the wall. The dog's head replicates the shape of a dog's favourite toy – a bone. In terms of rendering, a series of fine lines in harsh highlight and deep shadow reproduce the fur without having to paint every fine hair. Finally, the carefully rendered eyes give us a 'human' point of entry into an animal portrait.

1 Make a quick pencil sketch. Scan it into Photoshop and make a light colour sketch on a new Multiply layer, using highlights and shadows of a single dominant colour to 'spot' the main areas of light and dark. Consider how the main elements of the picture interrelate – the moonlight along the top of the dog and the wall, the dog's black nose echoing the position and colour of the black cat and the shadows under the muzzle.

2 Flatten your image and import the layer into Painter, which has a much wider spread of naturalistic tools and filters, the better to replicate the organic elements of the dog's hair. Start to build up the texture of the fur and the wet nose using a fine brush in a dark pastel or charcoal material. Use the Blending tools to massage the colour into the basic blue of your image, leaving your lines sharper the darker the colour gets.

3 Start to work in the other colours and compositional elements – paint in the base coat for the eyes and collar, and begin to block out the bushes and the back wall. Don't be afraid to go overboard on the smudging and blending of colours at this point – you want to create a variety in texture and tone within a limited palette, and will be tightening up each portion of the illustration at the final stage. Pay close attention to the shading around the eyes and mouth, and to the expressive eyebrows, which will need to stand out against both the mid-tones of the fur and the highlights.

4 More colours are added to vary the palette: deep blue-greens for the suburban hedges and a dark brown for the brickwork. The composition has also been tightened – where previously the moon was a crescent shining from the top left, it is now a full circle spotlighting the cat. The full moon echoes the white circles of the dog's eyes, drawing the viewer's attention to the cat. The image is imported back into Photoshop for some final fine brushwork on the eyes and nose. The foliage leaves are created from a custom brush set to blue/ green, and a brick texture added as a pattern fill completes the picture.

Sinister cat caricature

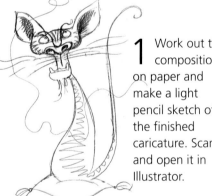

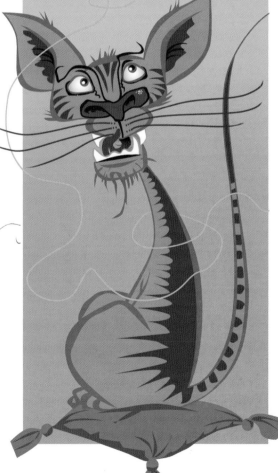

1 Work out the composition on paper and make a light pencil sketch of the finished caricature. Scan and open it in Illustrator.

2 Draw over the outline of the cat and its markings in colour using the Pen tool, varying the thickness as you go. Next, apply the flat colour fills on the layer beneath. Repeat this process for the purple cushion.

3 Fill in the eyes with a radial gradient of orange to white and add the black coils of whiskers. Add overlapping tufts of deep orange to the outer line to lend variety to the fur. On a new layer, create a gradated rectangle background, bleeding from orange to mauve. Finally, colour the fly in black and delineate the flight trail in a pale blue colour, using the Freehand Pen tool.

Final image

The elongated, top-heavy shape of this sinister cat provokes much amusement. The picture is anchored by background colours that reflect the cat and its environment, while the trail of the fly draws the image up and across the picture to its focal point. A simple image such as this would make a perfect Flash animation – simply moving the fly around the image with the cat's eyes following its course would be very effective.

Simple animation

Many simple Internet animations are created using Flash and it is ideal for anybody new to animation. It is designed to work in conjunction with vector and paint programs and they share common features, such as building images in layers. The different elements can either be created directly in Flash or in Illustrator or Photoshop and then imported.

   Although the animation is still very simple, it is easy to lose track with so many layers of moving parts, so the following projects have been broken down into easy-to-follow stages. There are three main ways in which to animate your illustrations: 'Motion Tweening', where Flash creates frames in between two keyframes that make an object movie; 'Shape Tweening', where Flash creates frames that cause one shape to morph into another; and 'Guided Motion Tweening', whereby a character or element moves along a set path. The following pages outline these methods in more detail.

Final animation

These sets of images comprise a very simple animation using two moving elements and a fixed background. However, it effectively demonstrates creating movement using keyframes, and some basic ways in which existing shapes – or Symbols, as they are called once converted to animatable components – can be moved, reshaped and made transparent.

Converting shapes to animated objects

Tip: The most common keyboard shortcuts in Flash are as follows:
F8: convert shape into Symbol
F5: insert new frame
F6: insert new keyframe
Enter: play movie
Ctrl + B: 'Break Apart' – if you have created an image with clearly defined parts, for example, a word, this function will break it apart into its component units – in this case, the letters. These can then be animated individually.

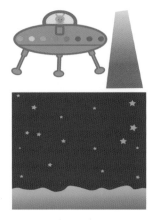

2 Our animation is of a spaceship taking off, a power beam extending underneath it. To create it, you will need to make a number of 'keyframes' at the key points of action. Flash will interpolate the animation between your keyframes. Click at frame 30 and press F5 to create 30 empty frames. To insert a new keyframe within those frames, click a point on the timeline and press F6, or right click and select 'Insert Keyframe'.

1 Create the spacecraft, beam and background in Illustrator, and import them into Flash as separate layers. Set the background as the background image, filling the whole of your frame. Change the spacecraft and beam into Symbols by pressing F8, or right-clicking and selecting 'Convert to Symbol'. Symbols are the moving parts in a Flash animation. Leave the background as it is.

3 Place the saucer on the ground at the bottom left of the frame, as shown, and hide the beam on the layer directly behind it. Now, add a new keyframe at frame 11 on the timeline. On this keyframe, select the saucer and move it directly up and into the middle of the picture. Extend the beam all the way down to the ground using the Transform tool. Select frames 1–11, click the Tween drop-down menu from the Properties toolbar and choose 'Motion'. This will create a smooth animation of the saucer rising into the sky, with the beam extending below it. Don't extend the slider bar of the beam past frame 11 when adding new frames – this will make it vanish at that point.

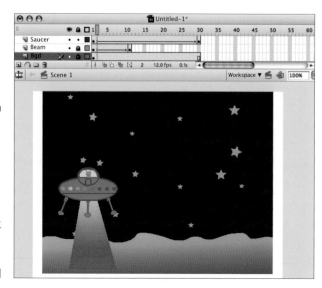

4 Create a new keyframe at frame 30, and move the saucer to the top right-hand side of the frame. Change the Alpha percentage of the saucer to 0% in the Colour Effect drop-down menu (Modify > Instance) – this will cause it to disappear by the time it reaches this frame. Press the Enter key on the timeline to preview your animation.

Motion tweening

3 Use the Transform tools to rotate the ear on frame 30. Now select frames 1–30 by clicking and dragging the mouse across them on the timeline, and click Tween > Motion. This will create a smooth motion between frames 0 and 30.

1 Create a simple image of a friendly dog in Flash or import the image from Illustrator, with the right-hand ear brought in as a separate layer. The higher the frame rate, the more convincing the quality of animation. To adjust the frame rate of the project, go to the document settings. Around 12 frames per second will achieve the best result.

2 Select the ear and make it into a Symbol (right click on the object and select 'Convert to Symbol', naming it 'Ear'.) On the timeline, create a new keyframe at frame 30 by right clicking on the timeline and selecting 'Insert Keyframe'. This creates a new frame with both the dog and the ear in the same position as they are at frame 0.

Final animation

This shows a very simple animation: a movement to a dog's ear. The ear is on a separate layer to the head and is made into a symbol. The ear is shown moving in two screengrabs: one shows the red 'onion skinning' outlines, the other the final effect. As well as movement, Flash allows you to turn one shape into another – in this example a green square into a mauve circle. Make further variations on the theme of the moving dog ear and morphing shapes and increase your ambition each time.

Shape tweening

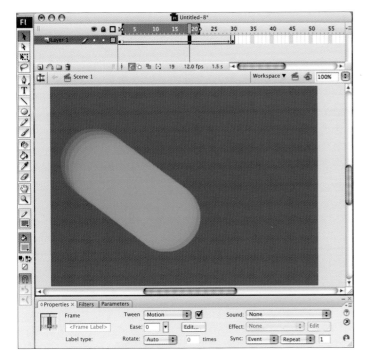

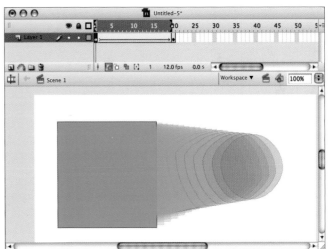

2 On this keyframe, select the green square and delete it. Draw a mauve circle using the Shape tool, again not converting it to a Symbol. Place it at the right-hand side of the frame. Now, select the frames on the timeline, click on the Tween drop-down menu in the Properties bar and select 'Shape'. Press Enter to see the square turn into a circle. You can loop this as a repetitive movement by selecting Control > Loop Playback.

1 Morphing one coloured shape into another can be achieved easily, as follows. Draw a green square with the Shape tool, but don't convert it into a Symbol, as you can only 'shape tween' between vector shapes. Place the square at the left-hand side of the frame. Using the F5 key and the timeline, create 30 frames of animation. Click at frame 30, and create a keyframe using F6.

Tip: Turning on 'onion skinning' by clicking the second button from the left in the timeline bar allows you to view previous frames in your sequence as 'ghosted' after-images on your current frame. This is useful for fine-tuning animations with the frame-by-frame method.

Advanced motion tweening and guided motion tweening

2 The screengrab on the right shows the library where every part of the dinosaur is named and saved as a Symbol to its own layer. The library can hold up to 16,000 symbols! Each Symbol should be saved as a Movie Clip (below), which is the top option in the dialogue box that appears when you select 'Convert to Symbol'. Motion tweening is used here in the same way that it is used on the previous spreads: to make the dinosaur walk, open its mouth and move its tail. However, whereas previously you were moving a single object from point to point using keyframes, you can now control several discrete objects, moving and scaling each one independently.

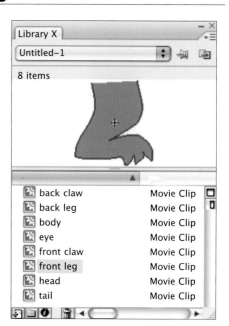

1 Create the component body parts. Either do this in Illustrator and import them as separate layers, or make them in Flash using the Shape tool. Save each piece of the body as a separate Symbol, which can then be moved and animated independently.

Final animation

This is a slightly more complex animation made up of eight moving elements, or Symbols. The background, being a fixed, flat image, can be created in one of two ways – as a photo, or in the same cut-out method as the dinosaur. While the dinosaur moves and opens its mouth like a pre-school picture book character come to life, an outsize prehistoric bee buzzes across the animation on a guided path.

Tip: Tracking progress is important, and you will need to stop and check how everything is coming together. When using Flash in particular, your timeline will not always offer a 'realtime' preview of your animation or interactive functions, and movie clips cannot be played unless in an exportable format. While you can create a final 'publish' of your Flash project, it's easier to publish a preview, which renders faster and opens in your Macromedia Flash project window. Simply go to File > Publish Preview, or press F12 on your keyboard (PC or Mac).

3 Here, the dinosaur is fully assembled 'on stage' in Flash, on an empty background. The screengrab on the right shows the empty timeline and layers before any animation or keyframes have been assigned, while the one underneath it, shows the slider bars and keyframes afterwards. Keyframes can be created for each individual component part, or you can move several components on a single keyframe. Learning to 'micro-manage' your animation in this way will give you the greatest control – and results.

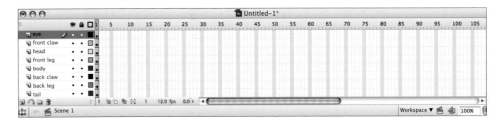

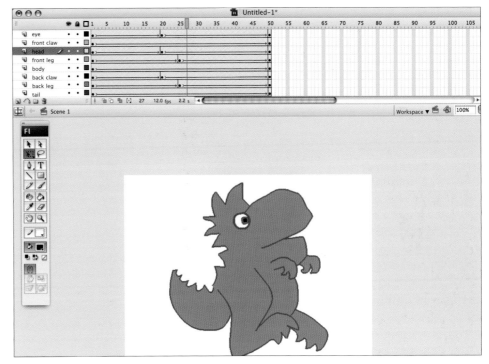

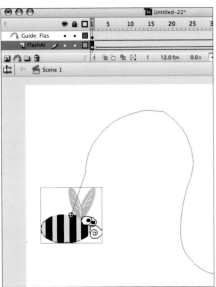

4 To create a background for the dinosaur (a non-moving, non-Symbol part), you can either create a flat background in Illustrator or Flash in the same style as your character, or import a digital photograph, as shown on the left. This stage can be added at any point, as it will not interfere with your animation.

5 The bee is the final element, here constructed in Illustrator, imported into Flash and saved as a Symbol. To make the bee move along a pre-determined path, do the following. Click the 'Create Guide' icon at the bottom of the layers menu (it's a blue cross and blue dot with a red dotted line joining them). Draw a wiggly path for the bee to follow on this layer. Click back to the bee's Symbol layer, select the Arrow tool and press the 'Snap to Objects' button in the Options area of the toolbox. Snap the bee to the guideline by moving it to the start of the line. Place the centre of the bee on the line (the centre will show as +). A black circle appears when the bee is snapped to the motion guide. Create a new keyframe at the end of the animation and snap the Symbol to the end of the line. Click the timeline and select Tween > Motion. The bee will now follow the guided path from beginning to end. Press Enter to see your completed animation.

Index